FLIPPING DIRT

By Mike Deaton

DEDICATION

To Ligia

I could not have conceived of a better partner on this journey.

In life, in love, in spirit, in entrepreneurship – across all the domains of life, you have inspired me to strive for more.

I love you so very much and here's to leaning in to more of this incredible journey together.

Contents

Chapter 1: The Sucker Punch – Losing Stability

This was the end. I knew it in my gut. The telltale signs I had orchestrated dozens of times and to thousands of employees before were all there: quick notice calendar invite, keyword: 'Mandatory,' HR in CC.

I was getting laid off.

How many times had I dodged this bullet before? Dozens? Some strategically, with foresight and careful repositioning; others, by sheer luck, navigating office politics, and delivering high performance; but I had always managed to stay afloat. Until now.

My number was up. Ticket punched. This was the end of the road. Time to face the music.

In truth, I had seen it coming. I had the conversation with my boss months earlier, and it was the right move—the only move. My team was geographically disconnected from HQ, operating from a shrinking office site, and we had been outsourcing operations for the past 18 months. The last thing I wanted was to relocate to Seattle, and if I'm being honest, I had even less desire to continue playing office politics in an increasingly cutthroat environment. "What have you done for me lately" is a stressful and fatiguing way to live life.

My personal job satisfaction was at an all-time low. Having been recently acquired by a larger company, my team and I were trying to integrate with a new corporate culture. Domestic and international travel consumed more than 50% of each month, and the relentless outsourcing of our supply chain to new suppliers while attempting to maintain service levels with inadequately documented processes was soul-crushing. I was exhausted.

So, when I heard a Reduction in Force (RIF) was coming, I made it clear that I wouldn't be upset to find myself on that list.

But here's the thing—no matter how prepared you think you are, when that moment arrives, you're never ready to hear, 'Your role is no longer required. Thanks for your service and contribution. HR will now walk you through your severance package.'

No matter how much you prepare, you're never ready for what comes next. I had sat on the opposite side of the conference table, whether real or virtual, countless times. I had seen a full range of responses – anger, shock, disbelief, despair. In those moments, as the blood rushes to your head, that throbbing whoosh fills your ears, and your mind races; you don't hear what HR is saying about supplemental benefits, job placement services, or any of that canned messaging. It's pure survival instinct. "How will I pay the bills?" "How will I provide for my family?" "How do I break the news to my wife?"

Speaking of which, that's where our story gets even more complicated.

Split screen:

While I was in a state of shock and half-listening to HR robotically run through all the 'benefits' I'd be receiving from being 'reduced,' my wife, Ligia had arrived for another day at the office with her healthcare company employer. Settling in to start her day, she noticed a few new faces in the office along with an unusual buzz of activity from the management team. Her standard morning was disrupted by a surprise team meeting and the announcement that the company needed to make some changes to remain competitive. Among those changes was the closure of the Plano, TX office (her office!) and a consolidation of those functions back to HQ in Fort Smith, Arkansas. More individual details would be covered in 1-on-1 meetings throughout the day.

WTF? What are the odds? On that day, for Ligia and me…apparently 100%.

That evening, neither of us could have foreseen the shock and despair of how to regroup, pay bills, and provide for our family, let alone how to navigate the lifestyle we'd enjoyed for years. I knew in my heart and head that we'd come out okay, but at what cost? How long would it take? What sacrifices would we have to make? This sucked. But what doesn't kill you makes you stronger, right? *Right!?*

The next few days were a flurry of activity – polishing up the resume, refreshing the LinkedIn profile, reaching out to recruiters, and working the network; all while ramping down a 15-year career and handing off activities to another team (a team that wasn't thrilled to take on more work by the way). Who knew getting let go could involve so much busy work?

I had a couple of quick wins on the job front, positions that seemed a good fit, plus a few connections at other companies were able to shop me around. This resulted in many calls and screening interviews with companies like Apple, Tesla, Amazon, and a few other tech leaders. And while this did serve to ease my anxiety a little on the employment front, I noticed an increase in unease in other areas of my psyche. All of these jobs were located on the West Coast, Midwest, or East Coast. None were in Dallas, or even Texas.

The thought of relocating, starting fresh at a new company, working with a new team and culture was not appealing in the least. On top of that, would I end up right back in the same miserable aspects of where I'd just been? A heavy travel schedule, office politics, bureaucracy, and tight budgets. Working my ass off in hopes of hitting the max annual salary increase of 4%? This sucked!

With each additional phone call and step taken deeper into the recruiting funnel, my sense of dread increased. I wasn't sleeping at night. My mind was constantly lit up with anxieties – thoughts of what each role might entail, how to make the best decision.

There had to be a better way…

Chapter 2: Seeds of Change – Discovering Real Estate

Rewinding many months from that crossroads moment, the seed of creating cash flow from real estate had been innocently planted and germinating in my mind. The reawakening wasn't purely coincidental in my subconscious.

When Ligia and I moved from Romania to the U.S. in 2010, we bought a home in Plano on a short sale. The bank was close to foreclosing on the house we would end up buying and was looking to sell at a discount. The current occupants had been remodeling the home and were unable to complete the work or pay the mortgage, so the house was in an unfinished state. This was on the back end of the Great Recession of '08, and many properties across the U.S. were just coming out foreclosures and being offered at deep discount levels.

Ligia and I loved the bones of the house and the amount of light inside. The fact that we could customize it as we wanted was also highly appealing. Our little taste of a fixer upper.

After completing work in the living spaces and the master bedroom, we moved on to updating the office with a new color scheme, some wood trim, new furniture, and bookcases. While unpacking a few boxes to finish out the room, I came across a familiar book—one cherished by almost everyone I speak to in the real estate space—*Rich Dad Poor Dad* by Robert Kiyosaki.

The purple book, as so many know it, is a simple yet powerful story about different ways to view money and investing. In summary, the book compares two approaches that largely reflect the way our society is structured: those that work for money, earning a paycheck and saving up for retirement; and those that put their money to work for them, owning businesses and investing to create cash flow. It's such a powerful story and one that clearly demonstrates how we can take control of our lives while leveraging our intelligence and creativity to build wealth.

Standing in the office of that Plano house, as I pulled the book out of the box from a stack of so many others, I remembered reading *Rich Dad Poor Dad* a few years prior while working and living in Romania. At that time, it had awakened a desire in me to find ways to create cash flow on the side. Rental properties had been on my mind, but I didn't feel comfortable with how or where to start;

or know how to buy something in Romania. Investing in property in the U.S. while living abroad also presented enough of a barrier that I hadn't pulled the trigger. However, it had stoked the idea of exploring options, be they real estate, businesses, or something else. As often happens though, life and work took over primary activities and those dreams of real estate slipped to the backburner.

Reigniting Old Flames

I'm a recreational runner and have been since about the time I turned 30. When we moved back to Texas in 2010, I signed up to run the Dallas Marathon. Having a big running goal gets me off the couch, out the door, and on my feet to train at least two days a week on longer runs of an hour or more, I had plenty of time to pop in the headphones and digest some content. My go-to listens were typically educational in nature, like audiobooks or podcasts.

During that time period, I was especially interested in business, investing, real estate, and other ways to create cash flow on the side. Pat Flynn's *Smart Passive Income* and *Side Hustle Nation* were a couple of my early favorites. It was during that time that I heard two different guests on two different podcast episodes share their stories of buying and selling vacant land to generate enormous profits and great cash flow. It intrigued me. The return on investment per deal averaged over 100%, and in some cases, up to 1000% - 10x! It compelled me. Compelled me to invest time in some online research and invest some money in educational material that promised to reveal just how to go about finding great land deals and flipping them for those alluring profits.

A few weeks later, that package arrived in the mail. Upon opening it, I discovered a few binders of printed material along with some DVDs to watch recorded video. Old school, lol! The internet was still in its early days of growth and online courses weren't so readily available. Excitedly, I put the material on my desk in the office, thinking I'd dive into it later.

Later turned into much, much later. Work, business travel, life, it all settled into its familiar groove, and left my land investing primer, my gateway to cash flow, just lying there, getting buried in dust…until life intervened and gave me one giant nudge – in the form of a layoff.

Chapter 3: The Dilemma

Corporate Offers vs. Entrepreneurial Dreams (2 Paths Diverged...)

I remember vividly after my second-round interview with the hiring manager at the largest retailer and logistics company in the world. "We have a few great openings coming up that you'd be perfect for," she said. "Cleveland. Des Moines. Birmingham. Even more hubs coming online quarterly." (in similar locations)

Ugh. Really? Relocation is one thing. But none of those places make my radar for ideal moves. I hung up the phone after a few pleasantries and no commitments. We could circle back later after conferring with Mrs. Deaton.

I was wrecked. Stomach in knots. Brain in a fog. Too many life decisions coming at me and none of them were a "hell yes!" Does that mean they're a "hell no!"?

I needed to clear my head. To wrap my thoughts around some path forward.

I needed to go for a cleansing run. Get a sweat going. Find the meditative rhythm of cadence and breath and let my thoughts untangle themselves to (hopefully) manifest some sense of clarity out of this.

Once back home, showered, and reenergized, my mood and thoughts were brighter. Sitting down with Ligia, we talked through our situation. It was clear that relocating to the West Coast, Midwest, or other options on the table were not our ideal scenario. We did have some savings and room to think about things. But if it meant survival and getting back into the workforce, we'd certainly pursue it. Maybe even enjoy a change of pace, get some income rolling back in and, in parallel, look for a transfer or job-hop to a preferred location.

My thoughts, however, kept telling me there was something better out there. Something that would be more fulfilling. More rewarding. Purposeful. But I couldn't quite make it out.

Ligia and I have a wonderful relationship with each other. There's a connectedness, understanding and sense of shared purpose – an ability to understand and pick up on cues and micro expressions that give insight into mood. We also have a way of interacting with one another that allows for, even encourages, open communication without fear of defensiveness, even in times of stress. It's a quality that I am truly grateful for and feel blessed for having found.

It was in these days together and through conversations and genuine openness that we were able to dig in deep. To discuss our hopes, our values, our desires for life. I have a strong coaching background, and it's one of the activities that really drives me in life. When I reflect on my corporate career as a leader and executive, the single most rewarding activity that I had during that time was coaching and mentoring others. Whether personal or professional, I love being able to listen to what's going on in a person's life, where they feel stuck, and helping move them forward. Watching my team develop, grow, get promoted, and succeed at their endeavors really drives me.

I'm also a personal development junkie. I have always had a thirst for performance improvement knowledge. I can remember discovering a box of Tony Robbins cassette tapes as a teenager and being blown away at the concept of being able to program our thoughts and behaviors to achieve results. Throughout my career, I loved to consume professional development books, articles, podcasts…you name it.

I'd also had the benefit of taking part in many corporate development courses and training programs during my professional career. As such, I had a large toolbox from which to work.

So, it was in that period of crisis and uncertainty that Ligia and I spent time working on our larger Purpose in life. Creating hierarchies and rankings of core values and sharing them with one another. We wrote out what our perfect day would look like. Created eulogy perspectives on important milestones we'd want to have achieved over the courses of our lives. Our own personal Life Coaching workshop. It was fun and liberating.

And nowhere in our exercises did relocation to the Midwest or working in an office or excessive business travel, office politics, or working someone else's agenda enter into the mix. Huh. Imagine that. Clues.

It was out of those exercises that we seriously began to wonder if a different way of life was possible. Could we do something radical? Chart an entirely new and different course with our lives? (We had such a limited mindset back then!)

We thought about…dreamed about a life on our own terms. Being free to choose our own direction and be in complete control of our time. My attention was drawn back to that dusty land investing binder that was on the desk in the office. We consumed its contents over the next two days. We were skeptical, but it sounded somewhat plausible. Easy even. Was it possible? Too good to be true? Other people seemed to have done it.

The course came with a pair of tickets to a weekend conference. We checked the dates for upcoming conferences, and the next one would be in San Antonio in a month. An easy drive from Dallas. We could do it. Drive down. Check out more information. Ask some questions and see what we thought.

We booked our hotel room and headed south a few weeks later. After two days of hype, exercises, stories, networking, and some fun in San Antonio, we decided to take the plunge. We'd go all-in and give it a shot.

Excitedly strategizing about our new course in life, we agreed to set some parameters around our new venture – allocating a lump of seed capital to get started and a 12-month timeline to make it work before reevaluating our situation and potentially changing direction. If this was really going to be our all-in, full-time path forward, we'd commit to invest in ourselves with training, education, and coaching. Reviewing a few different coaching packages and training options, we arranged calls to vet them out and take a decision.

Ultimately, we decided one-on-one coaching would serve us best. We wanted to accelerate the ramp-up period, minimize any potential risks, and leverage the expertise of those that were already successful. We both had to digest a five-figure sticker shock of signing up for personalized coaching. We both had our reservations, but Ligia was a confident cheerleader and had faith we'd easily earn back that investment through speed of implementation and avoidance of mistakes. Once we'd taken our decision, we put that concern behind us and got down to the business of…starting a business.

Having spent the recent decades running operations and supply chains in a corporate environment, my natural inclination and comfort zone was in setting up our strategy and startup approach. We scheduled the initial coaching appointments, structured our days, established key metrics to track progress, and eagerly digested educational material. It was a lot in the beginning, a firehose of information. Real estate was a new 'language' for each of us. Not a difficult one by any means, but new. In addition, as with any new skill, there were technical aspects that took learning and getting used to, such as spreadsheets, formulas, macros, and advanced operations. Frustrating at times but certainly manageable.

Our early days with our new business and coaching program were filled with ups and downs. We initially felt misled and overhyped. We were sold on the idea that we'd be coaching with the face of the brand, the Land Geek himself. In reality, we were assigned a 'senior coach.' Jumping on a clarification call with Mark, he assured us we were in better hands. However, after our first few calls with our initial coach, we were left unimpressed. He'd show up for our calls seemingly unprepared, needing the first five or ten minutes to get settled in, and then ask where we left off from the last lesson. Robotic. Clinical. Like that teacher in school who had superior skills in math, technically qualifying him as an expert in the subject, but lacking the ability to communicate it to those who didn't already understand the language…and not really interested to be doing it. This was all in addition to the lack of personality or personal check-in on how we were doing personally with the whole concept of being first-time entrepreneurs and tackling tasks we were not familiar with.

For the amount of money we were shelling out for this service, we wanted more. We expected more. We set up a call with Mark to discuss and shared our concerns. His response: "Yeah, I've heard similar feedback from other clients. It's not a total surprise. Let me see what I can do."

WTF?!? Why would you keep assigning someone to new clients that gets poor feedback?

Mark switched us to another 'senior coach,' and we started up again. After rebooting our experience, our results drastically improved.

We were excited during the business ramp-up period. We were learning, growing, optimistic, and taking action! We were defining and achieving small wins along the way, but had yet to make bigger progress, like a property sale.

We'd successfully built the foundation of land flipping. For us, that meant some company basics like setting up a company name and an LLC. Land flipping is so easy and can be run simply from a personal aspect; but we were looking to go full-time and long-term and wanted to present ourselves formally and enjoy the benefits and protection of an LLC.

Making offers and acquiring inventory land was our next step. We would do this as direct mail campaigns.

We created an offer letter template that we would use once we had a market selected and a list of property owners' names ready to go. And here's where we hit our first rough patch.

Going into the process, we leaned on the adage and guidance that you should invest in real estate 1) in your own backyard, 2) in a place where you have 'boots on the ground' that can help you assess opportunities, or 3) in a location you're already familiar with. All great advice for rental properties or other real estate asset classes. Not at all relevant for land flipping. But that was our starting point.

Flipping dirt can be done from anywhere and with land in any market. The availability of resources to help is a non-factor. Any insights or helpful information can be easily sourced online. As newbies to the business, we didn't have that knowledge yet and we didn't get that guidance from our coach.

We were living in Plano in the Dallas-Fort Worth market, so we decided to explore markets within a two-hour radius of the greater Metroplex. We initially settled on East Texas with its near endless acreage. I'm super analytical by nature and leaned into that. We looked at county websites for 'friendliness' factors:

- Land records: Did they have property owner names readily available? A downloadable tax roll? We called a few to see if they were open to share the tax roll or at least allow purchase of it. None of them acted like they knew what we were even talking about. Onward.
- Availability of tax information: Could we see who owed back taxes?

- Mapping: Some counties have a mapping program that allows you to see the property location, boundaries, details of the land use, and ownership.
- Sales information: Some counties will post sale data online. Texas, however, is what's called a non-disclosure state, so sale information is confidential.

We also checked a few of the online marketplaces for real estate and land like LandWatch, Land and Farm, and Lands.com to see what comparable properties in each of those markets were listed for.

Still, we really didn't know what we didn't know at this point and were following the roadmap and advice from our first coach, which was limited at this point.

He seemed to have some kind of reluctance in giving practical advice when it came to market selection.

- Too busy?
- Fear of overstepping?
- Letting the clients find their own path?

Not sure, and he wouldn't say. So, we soldiered on, testing different markets, learning, adjusting.

We had what we thought was early success: accepted offer responses being the measure of success at this point. But each time we dug in a little deeper into that initial phase of due diligence, we came away with either issues or uncertainty:

- Offer pricing not exactly right
- Back taxes accumulated above a practical level
- HOA dues accumulated more than the property value
- Zoning issues

We just weren't quite finding our sweet spot. Honestly, looking back, we were also full of doubt and uncertainty, afraid of making a misstep. We also hadn't dialed in our strategy in terms of the property we were looking for. We were focused on the challenges and not seeing the opportunities. All things we've made sure we incorporated into our own coaching program these days.

Regardless, we continued to plow through several East Texas markets before turning our attention to West Texas in hopes of striking paydirt.

Chapter 4: Striking Paydirt – First Successes and Lessons Learned

To strike paydirt when Flipping Dirt (aka find success), one of two things has to happen: you get lucky, or you get laser-focused on a successful plan. I've never been a big believer in hoping for luck but rather seeing as the intersection of preparation meets opportunity, as the saying goes.

We spent the first five months of our land journey applying lessons and learnings. We were heads-down and grinding. Two of us each working at least 40 hours a week. We explored multiple counties, sent out hundreds of offers to property owners, performed due diligence on dozens of properties, and invested thousands of hours in ramping up our business.

And while we'd made progress, we hadn't landed our first sale, which was incredibly frustrating! It was also getting to be demotivating.

We had made a few acquisitions however, consisting of:

- A Texas lake lot, which was a family property that my dad wanted to sell (pro tip: use whatever resources you can find)

- A heavily treed lot in a beautiful part of Colorado

We'd worked through and successfully ramped up the first part of the land flipping supply chain. Our acquisition deal flow was gaining momentum.

Now we needed to get that first sale under our belts.

And so, without letting up on the front end of the business, acquisitions, gaining that first sale became our predominant point of focus. To execute on getting that sale, we looked at all the variables such as, ad copy, marketing channels, ad volume, lead interaction, closing techniques, and pricing structures.

Marketing and sales in Flipping Dirt is not unlike other businesses.

Ad copy mirrors similar principles as other industries: speak to emotions like pain points, desires, hopes, and dreams; benefits over features; grab attention and hold it; entice taking that next step. Nothing fancy or overly complicated. Basics.

To find buyers in the land business, there are a wide variety of marketing channels that can be used. With our Flipping Dirt clients, we break these down into two categories: free and paid.

Free marketing channels that work well are the common ones of the internet, such as social media networks and online community platforms. Facebook and Craigslist have millions of users and localized groups specific to buying and selling. Zillow is a great real estate platform with buyers shopping for real estate. Even platforms such as Instagram, TikTok, X, and Threads can be used to market and sell property; but also, to build out your own list of leads.

Paid marketing channels in real estate can be great vehicles for selling land, even though many are crowded marketplaces with different 'tiers' determining how well your property will be promoted. A quick internet search will reveal the popular platforms of the moment. Some of the larger platforms you can find are:

- LandWatch.com
- Land.com
- LandFlip.com

Another channel we consider a paid marketing channel is real estate agents. Agents are great ways to leverage talents on a commission basis. They will do much of the heavy lifting to get a property sold: taking pictures, writing copy, listing it, showing it, working their network, fielding calls, and closing. They're also great resources to help with pricing and local market comps.

The trade-off is obviously a percentage of the sale (typically 6%-10%), which eats into any margin. So it's up to you, your goals and the amount of margin in your properties. Another type of trade-off, which you can see as a positive or a negative, is that agents usually bring in cash buyers. So, for quick cash flips, this is great. But it also limits your pool of buyers. If your goal is to line up an owner-financed deal and/or you want more potential buyers, then using an agent can be more challenging.

When we started our land business, our overarching goal was to build up passive income from 'note' payments that come through owner financing our sales to buyers. More details on the process of this later, but here I'll highlight the point that we let our goal steer us through many of these decisions such as which channels to market, how to price our properties for sale and what, if any help we leveraged. In our coaching programs, we lead with this strategy so that clients are clear on their goals and have the strategy to achieve those goals in the quickest and most efficient way possible.

Pro tip: Ultimately, out of all of these, one of your primary goals is to get qualified leads into your own database, even if they don't buy the exact property you have listed. Use a good CRM (Customer Relationship Management database) so that you have the ability to follow up via email and/or phone. We focused heavily on this to build up and leverage our own "VIP Land Buyers" list as a first option when selling (or even pre-selling!) properties. We can also use that list or database of interested land buyers to test markets and types of properties that our community is most interested in. It's a gold mine and we don't have to rely on black box algorithms or paid service providers' choices on who gets amplified…or not.

Real estate is incredibly powerful for wealth-building. It's also a very crowded marketplace, despite what you may think. So as with other products and services, you need to stand out. You must grab attention in this attention-based economy. That means in addition to great advertising copy and imagery, volume helps. The more advertisements (free and paid) in the more locations you can place ads for your properties, the better. There are several ways to go about this, which echoes a key reason why land is an amazing asset class – flexibility.

I'll touch on this later, but most, if not all, of the land flipping processes can be done yourself, with contract labor, using full-time employees, or even automated in many instances. So, whether you want to leverage sweat equity to get started and build up faster wealth or leverage the talents of others while saving your time, you can make it happen in the land business.

Ligia and I used many of these elements to grab that first sale. We worked across social platforms and websites, using different types of ads. We flooded the zone by joining different Facebook groups, Craig's List communities, refreshing ads to keep them at the forefront of feeds, and being responsive to any inquiries. And once that first sale did happen…we celebrated big time!

Our first sale was a watershed moment. We sold a small property in Texas – a parcel we acquired well below market value. It wasn't a huge moneymaker, but it was the proof of concept we needed. The sale confirmed that our efforts and learning were worth it. This first success gave us confidence in the business model. We gained increased competency across the processes. Learning by doing is really the best way to learn.

But the land-flipping business doesn't have to be just about quick flips; it can also be about building long-term cash flow.

Our entrepreneurial goal has always been to build a lifestyle built on financial freedom. To do that, we aimed to build up a portfolio of monthly recurring income. In the business of Flipping Dirt, this is achieved by owner-financing sales, often referred to as a "Note Portfolio" or simply "notes." This is because when buyers finance a land purchase through you, one of the legal documents used is a Promissory Note – a promise to pay monthly installments over time, like a car payment.

Having left the corporate world and W-2s behind, and without alternative sources of income, we were living on savings…and watching it reduce month over month as we ramped up our land business. It was anxiety-inducing, to say the least. And having built a career in Operations, I set up a series of goals along the way to our larger goal of financial freedom – a dashboard of key performance indicators, metrics and progressive milestones leading to that larger goal.

The next milestone along our journey after that first sale was getting our finances to the breakeven point so we could stop dipping into savings each month. As anyone in tune with operational finances knows, there are top and bottom lines – income and expenses. To give ourselves the best and quickest shot at success, we worked not only on the top revenue line, but also on the bottom-line expenses. We downsized where we could, tightening our belts and getting rid of unnecessary expenses so we could hit our goal faster.

The focus on recurring income through notes was not just a strategy; it was a necessity. We needed cash flow that could sustain us and grow over time. With each owner-financed deal, we added another layer of security to our financial future. It was methodical and steady progress. And sure, there were some challenges along the way, such as acquiring inventory, buyers defaulting (which is actually a benefit to the profit margins!), slowly stacking up note payments, and the occasional headache of clients that couldn't make payments and wanted to renegotiate. But every note added to our portfolio was a step closer to the freedom we sought. It was also exciting work to see progress toward our dream and build a business that enabled so much freedom.

As we gained more experience, we also began to refine our approach. We became more selective in the properties we purchased, focusing on land that had the highest potential for resale with favorable terms for owner-financing. We utilized services, such a system for managing our notes, using software that helped automate the process, track payments, and handle the administrative side of the business.

Over time, our note portfolio grew, and with it, our confidence. We were no longer just flipping dirt; we were building a sustainable, income-generating machine that could support the lifestyle we envisioned.

Reflecting on those early days, I realize that our success wasn't just about the strategies we employed or the deals we made. It was about the mindset we adopted – the relentless focus on our goals, the willingness to learn and adapt, and the commitment to seeing our vision through, no matter the obstacles.

Our journey into land flipping wasn't just a financial pursuit; it was a transformative experience that reshaped our lives. It taught us the value of resilience, the power of strategic thinking, and the importance of pursuing a life that aligns with our values and aspirations.

And as we continued to grow our business, we began to see that the possibilities were even greater than we initially imagined. Land flipping wasn't just a means to an end; it was the foundation of a new way of living – a life of freedom, flexibility, and financial independence.

With each new deal, we were not only building wealth; we were building the life we had always dreamed of. And that, in the end, is what made all the challenges and sacrifices worthwhile.

Chapter 5: Burn the Boats – Committing Fully to the Land Business

There comes a point in every journey where you have to make a choice: to fully commit or to keep one foot in and another out, wavering between comfort and the unknown. For us, that moment arrived with complete clarity.

The phrase "burn the boats" originates from a dramatic and decisive moment in history. In 1519, Hernán Cortés, the Spanish commander, arrived on the shores of the New World with his small army.

Facing overwhelming odds and a powerful enemy, Cortés made a bold move – he ordered his men to burn their boats, leaving them no possibility of retreat. The message was clear: they would either conquer and claim victory or die trying. There was no turning back, no safety net. With nothing to lose and everything to gain, Cortés's men fought with an intensity that led to their eventual triumph. The logic behind this radical strategy was simple: without the option to retreat, the only way forward was to succeed.

This story resonated with us deeply. Once we were laid off, free of the shackles of a salary, someone else's mission, and the illusion of corporate security; yet pulled by the need to earn an income, we knew we had to do something quickly. Thankfully, we took time to check in with our feelings, reassess our desires and align our life with our values.

For me, there was no additional thought given to straddling two worlds, no dipping our toes in the entrepreneurial water to see if the temperature was right. I knew we had to go all in. I had to burn the boats.

With our decision made, we looked forward to taking the plunge into the land business with everything we had. This wasn't just about exploring a new opportunity; it was about redefining our lives, about taking control of our future, and doing so with no safety net. The only way forward…was forward.

For us, taking the decision to fully commit meant reassessing our entire life to set up our new foray into entrepreneurship for the best chance of success. We sold our house in Plano, capitalizing on the hot DFW market, and decided to move to Boulder, Colorado – a place that called to us with its proximity to mountains, outdoor lifestyle, and sense of freedom. But this wasn't just a geographic relocation; it was a symbolic shift, a way of leaving behind the old life and fully embracing the new one. It was also a result of defining and ranking our Core Values. We needed to live our lives to the fullest and in that moment rather than spend more time working for an employer and delaying (or even forgoing) the adventures and lifestyle we wanted to enjoy.

Moving was an adventure. We packed our lives into a rental truck, gave away any possessions that didn't fit (the truck or our new lifestyle), said goodbye to friends and familiar places, and set off for Boulder with a mixture of excitement and trepidation. It was a fresh start, a clean slate, and we were determined to make the most of it.

Once settled in Boulder, we threw ourselves into the business with renewed energy and excitement. There were no more distractions, no more hesitations. Every day was about moving forward, whether that meant defining and refining our business processes, expanding our network, or simply grinding through actions and the inevitable challenges that come with any new venture.

One of the first things we did as new real estate entrepreneurs was to reexamine and establish new goals. We knew that success in the land business required more than just buying and selling property; it required a strategic approach, a long-term vision. We set clear milestones, such as quarterly and monthly income targets, extrapolated that into acquisition goals, and timelines for when we wanted to see certain results. The goal wasn't simply about making money; it was also about building something sustainable, something that could provide us with the freedom and flexibility we dreamt of and that we craved.

We also invested in our greatest assets – ourselves. We attended workshops, bootcamps, and webinars. We devoured books, consumed podcasts, and sought out mentors and communities who could guide us along the way. Every piece of information, every new skill, was another tool in our arsenal. We weren't just busily running a business; we were ensuring we developed entrepreneurial skillsets and honed our craft in order to hit our goals.

In addition to all building blocks, there also came "real work" – the day-to-day grind that separates those who succeed from those who abandon their dreams. We spent hours analyzing different markets, sending out offers, negotiating deals, and marketing and selling the properties we had already acquired. It was exhausting at times, and certainly there were moments of doubt when we wondered if we had made the right choice. But we kept going, driven by the vision we had for our future.

"When you have a why, you can bear any how."
– Viktor Frankl

We also leaned into the importance of discipline. In the corporate world, there are structures and systems in place to keep you on track. As entrepreneurs, especially in something as self-directed as land flipping, you have to create those structures for yourself. We developed daily routines, set up blocks of focus time, and held ourselves accountable to the goals we had set. Discipline wasn't just a nice-to-have; it was an essential element of success. As a husband-and-wife team, we thankfully have an incredibly supportive way of interacting with each other. But honestly, as accountability partners, we can be a little soft on one another. Here we had to make a pact and really help each other push through obstacles and resistance so that we stayed on track.

As the weeks passed, our efforts really began to pay off. We started closing more deals, building a portfolio of properties and land notes that generated consistent income. The milestones we had set—$1,000 a month, $10,000 a month, our first $50,000 month—came and went, each one a testament to the power of commitment and hard work.

We took time to celebrate! From the many small wins along the way, to the bigger milestones, we made sure to let those moments sink in reinforced them with celebrations.

But more than anything, this chapter of our journey taught us the incredible freedom that comes from having control. As an employee, you're always at the mercy of someone else—your boss, the boss's boss, even the whims of clients. But in this new life, we were in control. We decided where to invest our time, our money, and our energy. We were building something that was ours; something that no one could take away; and, most importantly, something that we created and controlled.

Looking back, I realize that burning the boats wasn't just about committing to the business; it was more importantly about committing to ourselves, to the life we wanted to live. It was about taking control of our future, about deciding once and for all that we were going to be the ones steering the ship.

As we continue to grow and evolve on this incredible journey, I reflect on that decision every day. It certainly wasn't the easy choice, but it was the right one. And it's made all the difference in our lives. I express gratitude literally each and every day for the decision we took, the life we've created and the fruits we enjoy.

Chapter 6: Taking Control of Your Income – The Illusion of the Traditional Retirement

The idea of traditional retirement is deeply embedded in our society as a time after which you work for decades; save and invest in stocks and bonds; and then you can finally relax, enjoy the fruits of your labor, and live off a steady pension or retirement fund. I can remember each of my grandfathers working for large corporations, finally having that retirement party, and then formally retiring. But in today's world, this notion is increasingly becoming an illusion. The security of a steady job and a pension at the end of the road is no longer a given. Today’s corporate entities have little to no allegiance to employees. Employees jump from company to company, or they work as contractors. Pensions are pretty much unheard of unless you’re a government employee, like teachers (my mom), military or other government agencies.

Add all of that into a situation where social security is under threat each and every year and retirement age is pushing closer and closer to 70, the prospect of exactly how to survive those golden years becomes difficult calculus. The reality is that to truly ensure your financial future, you must take control of your income (especially the upside potential), diversify your sources of wealth, establish cash-flowing assets, and build a safety net that you control.

Personal Financial Protection – Your First Line of Defense

The first step in taking control of your income is ensuring your personal financial protection. What this means is always striving to have at least a six-month emergency cushion. Life is unpredictable, and you never know when you might face an unexpected expense, a sudden job loss, or a downturn in the market. Having that financial cushion gives you the breathing room to handle emergencies without derailing your long-term financial goals.

Another key aspect of personal financial responsibility is managing debt. Here I refer to personal debt such as credit cards, personal loans that don't generate cash flow and even your home if you carry a mortgage. All of these are controllable. All of these can also intensely burden your ability to grow and build wealth and prepare for the future.

For us, having a safety net and minimal expenses was a non-negotiable factor during our startup phase. We made it a priority to build and maintain this cushion as well as operational contingency funds while we transitioned away from salaries and into our land business.

But we didn't stop there. We also focused on creating assets that would generate passive income. At this point, we focused specifically on selling land deals with owner financing that built up a "note" portfolio (clients that were paying us over time for their land purchase, like a car loan or mortgage). This approach allowed us to build a stream of income that wasn't dependent on our daily efforts. These payment terms were five years on average. This meant if something happened in our day-to-day lives or if we wanted to take some time off or pivot into other businesses, money would continue to come in month-over-month. It was our way of ensuring that no matter what happened, we had financial protection in place. And that safety net and cash flow stream equaled stress-free living.

Cash Isn't King…Cash FLOW is King

In the world of financial freedom, there's a popular saying that "cash is king." And while having cash on hand certainly has its advantages, it's not the ultimate key to unlocking a life of freedom and opportunity. The true ruler of financial independence is cash flow – a consistent and steady flow of income that doesn't rely on selling assets or depleting savings. Cash flow is what gives you the freedom to make choices, take risks, and live a life that aligns with your values and dreams.

Think about it this way: cash is finite. If you have a lump sum sitting in your bank account, you can spend it, but once it's gone, it's gone. It may be a nice safety net (and you should have a safety net!), but it's not working for you. You may enjoy 1% or so in interest, but that's not keeping up with the cost of living. And once you've depleted it, you're back to square one, needing to generate more.

Cash flow, on the other hand, is recurring income. It's the paycheck that keeps coming in, month after month, regardless of whether you're actively working or not. When you have a reliable cash flow, you don't have to live with the constant fear of running out of money. You can make decisions with the confidence that more income is coming in, allowing you to plan for the long term, rather than always scrambling for short-term solutions.

This steady flow of income means more than just covering your bills. Cash flow gives you the power to take control of your time, pursue the projects that excite you, and say "yes" to opportunities without financial hesitation. When your expenses are consistently met through cash flow, you're free from the "feast or famine" cycle that so many people experience. Instead of worrying about making ends meet or wondering how long your savings will last, you're in a position to grow, expand, and invest in your future. This shift, from worrying about running out of money to knowing you have a dependable source of income, creates a sense of security and freedom that pure cash simply can't provide.

With cash flow, you also gain the flexibility to weather life's ups and downs without tapping into your reserves. Let's face it: unexpected expenses and opportunities will always come up. Medical emergencies, family needs, or even the chance to invest in a business venture, all of these require funds. If you're relying solely on a cash reserve, those expenses quickly drain your resources. But with cash flow, these life events are merely bumps in the road, not financial disasters. You're not forced to dip into savings or liquidate investments; instead, your steady income stream can absorb these fluctuations, keeping you on track toward your goals.

In the context of flipping land, building up cash flow rather than one-time profits becomes even more essential. Imagine creating a portfolio of land notes – income-producing land deals where buyers make regular payments to you over time. This is a powerful way to build a passive income stream that works for you. Each deal adds to your cash flow, moving you closer to financial independence, without requiring you to sell off more assets or trade more hours for dollars. Land flipping can start with one-time sales, but transitioning into cash-flowing deals can unlock a whole new level of financial freedom and sustainability.

Ultimately, cash flow is about freedom – freedom to work on your own terms, to pursue your passions, and to live life without the constant worry of running out of money. Cash flow is what separates those who are merely rich from those who are truly wealthy because wealth is not measured by a single sum but by a system that keeps giving back to you. When you focus on cash flow over cash, you're building a life that's resilient, adaptable, and capable of sustaining your dreams in the long term. In the end, it's this steady flow of income that becomes the true king, paving the way for a life filled with choice, security, and endless possibilities.

The Importance of Diversification

Once you've established a solid financial foundation and built a cash-flowing engine, the next step is diversification. It's critical to stability and long-term success. Our story is a testament to this. We started with two incomes from (what we thought were) stable corporate jobs, but when the layoffs came, we quickly realized how much we had relied on those employers. Health care, income, benefits, the loss of income was a harsh wake-up call. We had spent years thinking about other possibilities, but we never took action. It wasn't until we were forced into a corner that we finally saw the importance of and took the decision to diversify our income streams.

I say this all the time, but today, there has never been a better time to take control of your income. The digital universe, Internet Revolution and now, AI Revolution, offers near-unlimited tools and opportunities to create, market, and sell digital products. Real estate remains a solid option for generating income, whether through rental properties or land deals like the ones we pursue. Side hustles are easier to start than ever before.

Heck, main hustles are easier than ever before to start. And the global reach of the internet means that your customer base is not limited by geography, and you can even market and reach them for free! It is truly incredible.

This abundance of opportunities means that you can diversify your income streams in ways that align with your interests and strengths. Whether it's through digital products, real estate, or other entrepreneurial ventures, diversification provides the stability needed to weather any economic storm.

Why You Need Control Over Your Income

The benefits of controlling your income go far beyond financial security. The illusion of safety with a W-2 job is just that—an illusion. I've spoken to countless people who were blindsided by layoffs, despite years of loyal service to their employers. The statistics on layoffs are sobering, and they highlight the importance of not relying solely on a single source of income.

As entrepreneurs, Ligia and I now feel a level of control that we never had in our corporate jobs. We know that more effort equals more results. But it's not just about working harder; it's about working smarter. Our aim is not to work harder. *Better* effort leads to better results. We have the freedom to choose whether we work solo or with a team, and we have the flexibility to pivot and diversify into alternative ideas and income streams as the market changes.

This control over our income allows us to live a life of empowerment. It gives us the confidence to face the future, knowing that we are not at the mercy of an employer or a volatile job market. Instead, we are in the driver's seat, steering our financial future in the direction we choose.

Chapter 7: Why Land? The Case for Investing in Vacant Land

When it comes to real estate investing, most people think of flipping houses, buying rental properties, or even getting into commercial real estate. But there's an often-overlooked asset class that offers some of the most compelling opportunities: vacant land. Investing in land has a unique set of advantages that make it a low-risk, high-reward strategy, particularly for those looking to get started in real estate with minimal investment costs and far less competition. Let me break down these and a few other reasons why land is such an attractive investment.

Low Cost of Entry (and the Lowest Risk Profile)

One of the most appealing aspects of land investing is the low cost to get started. Literally anyone can get started in land. You can get started with Unlike other forms of real estate that require significant upfront capital, we've been able to purchase land for as little as $99. Yes, you read that right—$99. And those ended up some of our best performing deals (on a percentage basis). This means that almost anyone with a small amount of capital can get started. We actually even helped a few clients get started with no money. There are ways to leverage your time and hustle to generate cash flow (more on that later!).

In addition to the low cost of acquiring some properties, the overhead to run a land business is incredibly low. You don't need to worry about legal fees, Title companies, brokers, property management, tenants, or costly repairs. The simplicity of the business model keeps ongoing expenses to a minimum, allowing for a lean operation that maximizes profit margins. The bulk of the costs are in acquisition – reaching out to landowners (there are a variety of means) and then buying properties.

Perhaps most importantly, we've never lost money on a land deal. This isn't just luck; it's the result of using a disciplined strategy to buy at the right prices.

There's an adage in real estate: you make your money on the buy. In the Flipping Dirt business, it is THE primary principle. Buying at the right price and under current market value allows an immediate profit to be generated – a huge one typically. There is no need for value-added renovations, appreciation or quite frankly, anything. You simply remarket, sell, profit and repeat.

And by following basic due diligence processes that we've established over time, we've been able to eliminate many of the other risks that can trip up other real estate investors. We know what to look for, what to avoid, and how to structure deals in a way that protects our investment. There simply aren't the other variables involved as there are in other asset classes that depend on occupancy, rent rates, repair allocations, interest rates, utilities, insurance rates or any of the other myriad factors that can negatively affect investments. Simple. Clean. Easy.

Abundance

One of the reasons land is such a great investment is the sheer abundance of it. There are quite literally millions of acres of vacant land across the United States, and with it comes a vast number of opportunities. You have access to hundreds of thousands of parcels of land, owned by individuals and entities who, for various reasons, are often motivated to sell but haven't listed their properties. Real off-market opportunities.

And the diversity of these opportunities is staggering. There are thousands of counties and markets to work in, each with its unique characteristics and advantages. Whether you're looking for desert plots, forested land, agricultural acreage, or suburban lots, there's no shortage of options. This abundance means that there's always a deal to be found, and with the right approach, you can continuously grow your portfolio.

We began our land investing journey in Texas – a state with a tremendous amount of land. From metro areas, suburban areas in the path of growth, to rural acreage, Texas has a "lot" to offer (pun intended). After feeling around and finally finding our own success in West Texas, we decided to focus on land in Colorado. We flipped incredible deals in Texas and still have clients paying off West Texas land. We simply resonate more strongly with mountains, pine trees and elevation. Our belief was that buyers and clients pick up on our energy in the sales process and we have a higher conversion rate. It's likely not the case, but that's compelled us to keep 80% of our focus on the Colorado markets.

The point is, we have, and you can, choose to find success in a wide variety of markets and property types because of the amount of land and land buyers. And the near-endless supply of deal flow also means that you're not competing with the same intensity found in other real estate markets, such as rentals and retail. This brings us to another significant advantage of land investing…

Low Competition

Compared to house flipping, multifamily syndications, or commercial real estate, the competition in the land business is very low. While these other asset classes are saturated with investors, land remains relatively under the radar. This low level of competition makes it easier to find and close deals without the pressure of bidding wars or aggressive negotiations. That's not to say there aren't other land flippers out there. We bump into them now and again and we hear from prospects that they have other offers. That's ok! Competition is a good thing. It's a sign of a healthy marketplace and also keeps us running a professional operation. I can't tell you the number of deals we've secured simply because we were the business that responded to an owner.

If you're in any kind of business, heck, even if you're an employee, then you are facing competition and have to take action to outshine and rise above. It's the beauty of capitalism.

Simplicity

On top of everything, land investing doesn't require the same network of partnerships, lawyers, brokers, lenders, or other critical elements that are essential in commercial or residential real estate. The simplicity of land transactions means that it's very approachable and quick to start, even for beginners. You can operate independently, without needing to rely on a large team or complex financing arrangements. This autonomy is incredibly empowering and allows for a streamlined, efficient business model.

Massive Return on Investment

Finally, and most importantly for us, the returns on land investments can be nothing short of extraordinary. We aim for a minimum of 100% return on investment. To be able to double our money in a short amount of time. We can do this because we'll only buy most properties if we can get it at 50% of the market value or less. This is entirely possible! Now depending on the size of a deal, we'll accept a tighter margin if it means a higher gross profit. For instance, if we're buying a property that would sell at market for $40,000 and we can buy it for $30,000 to net $10,000 in profit, even though we won't double our money, we also won't turn down $10,000!

But over the years we've been in business we've averaged almost 200% annualized returns. But it doesn't stop there. On some deals, we've made 1000% or more, and in a few cases, we've achieved infinite returns on our investments (on a percentage basis, not actual dollars, although that would be the ultimate deal).

These kinds of returns are virtually unheard of in other real estate asset classes, at least with any kind of consistency. We've invested in plenty of other types of real estate ranging from short-term rental properties up through large-scale commercial real estate. And while those investments can be profitable, they come with higher risks and often don't meet our return expectations. They also carry the weight of an incredible amount of stress and hassle-factor. Land, on the other hand, has consistently delivered exceptional returns, making it a cornerstone of our investment strategy. It also is virtually stress-free. We joke with each other that “there are no land emergencies!” No midnight calls about broken pipes or damage from tenants. Just peaceful, steady cash-flow.

Chapter 8: What You Need to Be Successful

Success in any field, whether it's sports, business, or real estate, is rarely about luck. It's about having the right mindset, the right skills, and most importantly, the right attitude. Over the years, I've learned that there are a few key traits that are essential for success in the land business—or any business, for that matter. These traits are tenacity, grit, coachability, and a commitment to the simple but powerful process discipline. In land, this formula consists of quite simply buying low and selling high.

Tenacity

Tenacity is the quality that keeps you going when things get tough. It's about persistence, determination, and the refusal to give up, no matter how many obstacles you face. In the world of real estate, tenacity is crucial. Deals fall through, markets shift, and unexpected challenges arise. The difference between those who succeed and those who don't often comes down to the one who is willing to stick it out, even when the going gets tough.

Take the story of Thomas Edison, one of the greatest inventors of all time. Edison is famous for his tenacity, especially in the development of the electric light bulb. It's said that he failed over 1,000 times before finally creating a working prototype. When asked about his many failures,

Edison famously replied, "I have not failed. I've just found 10,000 ways that won't work." His relentless pursuit of success, despite countless setbacks, is a perfect example of the power of tenacity.

In the land business, you'll face your share of challenges—deals that don't go as planned, properties that don't sell as quickly as you'd hoped, and buyers who back out at the last minute. But if you're tenacious, if you keep pushing forward despite the obstacles, you'll find that success is just around the corner. It's not about never failing; it's about never giving up.

When we started out, we faced our share of misses. I've mentioned them before, but we hit areas with high back taxes, higher HOA dues accumulated and those with low response rate. But we persisted, were tenacious and found markets that worked great.

Grit

While tenacity is about persistence, grit takes it a step further. Grit is a combination of passion and perseverance—it's about working hard over long periods of time, maintaining your focus and enthusiasm even when progress is slow. It's the ability to sustain your efforts and stay committed to your goals, even when the results aren't immediate.

The concept of grit was most recently popularized by psychologist Angela Duckworth, who studied high achievers in various fields. She found that grit, more than talent or intelligence, was the key predictor of success. People with grit are those who stick with their goals for years, not just weeks or months. They are willing to put in the hard work, day after day, year after year, to achieve their long-term objectives.

In business, grit is essential. Consider the story of Howard Schultz, the former CEO of Starbucks. Schultz grew up in a poor neighborhood and faced numerous challenges on his path to success. When he first proposed the idea of selling high-quality coffee in a chain of cafes, he was met with skepticism and rejection. But Schultz had grit. He believed in his vision and worked tirelessly to bring it to life. Today, Starbucks is a global brand, and Schultz's story is a testament to the power of grit.

One of Ligia's favorite business role models is Sarah Blakely. Sarah created a super popular women's fashion product known as Spanx. They are slimming undergarments that fit well and function better. Sarah has an incredible story of her entrepreneurial journey that ranges from designing the product, getting anyone to manufacture it and then working tirelessly to get it on retail shelves. She also has an incredible childhood training with parents who encouraged trying new things, not succeeding and still being proud of the effort in trying something new. That carried Sarah and her business through difficulties and into the multi-billion-dollar brand it is today. That is a testament to the power of grit.

In the land business, grit means staying committed to your long-term vision, even when the road is bumpy. It means continuing to invest in your education, developing your skills, refining your strategies, and putting in the work, even when the rewards are not immediate. Success in real estate doesn't happen overnight, but with grit, it will happen.

Coachability

No one achieves success alone. Even the most successful people in the world have had mentors, coaches, and advisors who helped guide them along the way. In fact, I would argue, *especially* the most successful people leverage coaches and mentors. Being coachable means being open to feedback, willing to learn, and eager to improve. It's about recognizing that you don't know everything and that there is always room for growth.

In sports, coachability is often the difference between a good athlete and a great one. Michael Jordan, widely considered one of the greatest basketball players of all time, was known for his coachability. Despite his immense talent, Jordan was always willing to listen to his coaches, take their advice, and work on improving his game. His willingness to learn and adapt, even at the peak of his career, is what set him apart from other players.

In the business world, coachability is just as important. When Ligia and I first started our land business, we sought out mentors who had already achieved the kind of success we were striving for. We knew that we had a lot to learn, and we were eager to soak up as much knowledge as possible. By being coachable, we were able to avoid many of the common pitfalls that new investors face and accelerate our path to success.

But coachability isn't just about listening to others—it has to be combined with taking action on what you've learned. It's essential to apply the advice you receive, test new strategies, and be willing to change course when necessary. The best coaches in the world can't help you if you're not willing to put in the work. Coachability is about being a lifelong learner, constantly seeking out new knowledge, and being willing to evolve as you grow.

Discipline: Buy Low, Sell High – The Simple Formula for Success

At the end of the day, all successful investing boils down to one simple formula: buy low, sell high.

This principle is as old as time, and it's the foundation of success in the land business.

In real estate, this means finding properties that are undervalued, purchasing them at a low price, and then selling them at a higher price to generate a profit. It sounds simple, but executing this strategy effectively requires a deep understanding of the market, careful due diligence, and a willingness to take calculated risks.

Warren Buffett, one of the most successful investors of all time, has built his entire career on the principle of buying low and selling high. Buffett's approach is to invest in undervalued companies with strong fundamentals, hold onto those investments for the long term, and sell them when they have appreciated in value. His success is a testament to the power of this simple yet effective strategy.

One of my favorite Buffett Maxims is:

Rule #1: Never Lose Money!

Rule #2: Never Forget Rule #1

In the land business, we've applied this same principle to great effect. By carefully researching markets, identifying undervalued properties, and negotiating deals that allow us to buy at the right price, we've been able to consistently achieve high returns on our investments. The formula may be simple, but its application requires skill, knowledge, and discipline.

Chapter 9: Finding Dirt Cheap Land to Flip

When it comes to real estate, the term "dirt cheap" couldn't be more literal when referring to the niche of land flipping. The allure of acquiring a property for less than the cost of a night out on the town is undeniable, but the true value lies in knowing how to navigate this market effectively. In this chapter, I'll walk you through the process of finding dirt cheap land, from selecting the right markets to making contact with property owners. Success in this field comes down to numbers, strategy, and consistency.

Selecting a Market or Markets

The first step in finding dirt cheap land is selecting the right market. Not all markets are created equally and understanding where to look can mean the difference between a profitable investment and a sunk cost.

- **Insights from Experience**:
    - **Southern U.S. States**: These areas often have vast tracts of land, both rural and residential, with numerous vacant parcels.
    - **Pacific Northwest**: Known for its natural beauty, this region offers unique opportunities for recreational land and rural residential properties, which can appeal to a specific buyer demographic.

    - **Midwest**: The heartland of America is dotted with rural properties, often selling at very low prices due to less competition and lower demand.
- **Keys to Successful Markets**:
    - **It's a Numbers Game**: Land flipping is a numbers game. The more you understand the numbers of your markets (submarkets and market comps), the better your chances of finding profitable deals.
    - **Plenty of Vacant Land**: It's best to look for markets where vacant land is abundant. Check county government websites for available land and public records. You can also do research using online real estate sites and platforms.
    - **Active Buying and Selling**: A healthy market is active. Monitor online sales sites and check county

sales records to see where activity is happening.

- **Competition as Validation**: A bit of competition isn't bad—it's a sign that the market is alive and property is in demand. If people are buying and selling land on platforms like Facebook, LandWatch, eBay, or Craigslist, that's a great indicator of a viable market.

- **Tips for Filtering Data**
  - **Price Bands**: Determine the price range you're comfortable targeting. For example, focus on properties listed between $5,000-$10,000 or $50,000-$100,000. Remember, your ultimatum is to pay less than the asking prices.
  - **Types of Land**: Decide on the type of land you want—recreational, commercial, agricultural, etc.

- **Location**: An easy filtering option, especially when you're getting started. It's always good to do some research on the submarkets within a larger market as price variation can be substantial.

Unearthing the Property Owners

Once you've selected your market, the next challenge is finding out who owns the land. With so much land out there, this task can seem daunting, but it's all about following the money.

- **The Ultimate Source: The Tax Man**
    - Regardless of what you may think, the US Government ultimately owns the land. We just rent it – in the form of taxes.
    - And since every piece of land is taxed, and the government knows exactly who will be paying those

taxes. Start by checking with the county tax collector—they have the records you need. It's merely a question of how easy they do or do not make it.

- **Owner Details**
  - **County Records**: Some counties have online databases where you can search for property owners. If that's not available, you might call the county directly. Ask them if they provide a list of the tax roll. Or if you're hyper focused, you can request a delinquent tax roll (although the full tax roll of vacant landowners is far more valuable).
    - **Pro tip: make sure if they have something that you know the exact data you need (name, address, acreage, valuations) and how you want**

it formatted (pdf, Excel, CSV…)

- **Third-Party Providers**: Companies like DataTree, PropStream and several others offer services to help you find and download targeted lists of property owners, often with additional insights like whether they are out-of-state owners or if they owe back taxes. You'll have to pay for these services, but it's often worth it from a convenience standpoint.
- **Alternatives**:
  - **Tax Deed Auctions**: Counties sometimes sell properties that have been foreclosed due to unpaid taxes. Be aware that some properties come with restrictions, like a seven-year waiting period before you can

resell. Contact the county directly to get the details.

- **Wholesale Marketplace**: The land flipping industry has a thriving wholesale market where you can buy and sell land. And while you'll sacrifice some profit margin, it may be worth it to you depending on your available resources and business goal.

Making Contact

After identifying potential properties and their owners, the next step is making contact. This can be done through various marketing approaches, and preparation is key.

- **Getting Prepared**
    - **Organize Your Data**: You'll need to arrange the information you've

gathered—property identifiers, owner names, mailing addresses, and potentially phone numbers and emails.

   - **Filter Your Data**: Who exactly will you be reaching out to? Considerations such as the location, value of the property, size of the property, location and type of owner are different ways to streamline your dataset and target your list.
   - **Clean Up Your List**: Remove duplicates, fix any incorrect addresses, and decide if you want to exclude certain owners (e.g., out-of-country, LLC's, Government agencies, etc.).

- **Approaches to Making Contact**
   - **Indirect Marketing**:

- **Online Ads**: Think of ads like "We Buy Ugly Houses" but tailored for land.
- **Social Media**: Establish a presence on platforms where you can engage with potential sellers.
- **Online Communities**: Join real estate and land communities where buying and selling occur regularly.
- **With indirect channels, you may be able to eliminate some of the steps above as it's not dependent on exact details like the owner's name or address**.

- **Direct Marketing**:
  - **Snail Mail**: Send postcards or letters to convey your offer. You can choose to be very

general to gauge seller interest or you may include an actual dollar amount for an offer on their property. Presenting an actual dollar amount often yields faster responses and more interested buyers. Leaving vagueness can net more initial responses, but you'll have to work harder in the negotiation phase since there is no expectation already set.

- **Texting**: There are services that can help with this but be mindful of FCC compliance issues.
- **Direct Phone Calls**: Another option, though it also comes with compliance requirements and getting those phone

numbers is more challenging than actual addresses.

The Goal

Your ultimate goal is to get offers in front of as many landowners as possible. This is a numbers game and in addition to volume, consistency is key.

Summary and final tips:

- **Aim for Consistency**: The power of consistency cannot be overstated. The more you reach out, the better your chances of landing deals.
- **Define Your Contact Options**: Always give owners multiple ways to reach you—phone, email, and mail.
- **Allow Room for Counteroffers**: Sometimes the seller will come back with a

counteroffer. Be open to negotiation but know your limits.

- **Measure Results**: Track your progress, analyze what's working and what's not, and adjust your approach as needed.

Chapter 10: The Protective Power of Due Diligence

In the world of land flipping, due diligence (DD) is your armor. It's what stands between success & profits and a bad deal. It's the process step that ensures you don't just survive in this business—you thrive. I've always said that land flipping is one of the safest forms of real estate, but that's only true if you do your homework. And by homework, I mean due diligence.

The Value of Due Diligence

Before diving into any deal, there are a few critical questions you need to answer:

1. **Is this actually a good deal?**
   - Not every piece of land is worth your time or money. You need to confirm that the deal is as good as it looks on paper initially. This is a quick go:no-go assessment and is largely based on price and basic ownership details.
2. **Should I buy this property?**
   - This isn't just about the price tag. You need to consider everything from location to future resale potential. Just because a piece of land is cheap doesn't mean it's worth buying. But I will say I will buy any piece of land for the right price.
3. **If so, what's the right purchase price?**

- Even if you've determined that the property is worth buying, what's the maximum amount you should pay? This ensures your profit margin remains healthy.

4. **Is my investment safe?**

    - Due diligence is the safety net that protects your capital from being sunk into a bad investment. It's the process that ensures your hard-earned money is going into something that will pay you back.

5. **Is it possible to lose my shirt?**

    - Land flipping can be a goldmine, but without proper due diligence, it could also be a pitfall. You don't want to end up with a piece of land that's more trouble than it's worth.

Execute Due Diligence in Two Phases

To make due diligence more manageable (and effective), go about it as a two-phase process. I'll highlight here and detail more just below.

1. **Initial Screening (Deal-Breakers)**
   - This is the first line of defense. It's the quick evaluation that helps you decide whether the property is even worth pursuing further. It's about identifying immediate red flags that could derail the deal before you waste too much time or resources. This is the Go:No-Go step.
2. **Final Due Diligence (Deal Makers)**
   - Once a property passes the initial screening, it's time to dig deeper. This phase is about confirming all the details and ensuring that everything checks out before you finalize the purchase and send payment.

Systems and Tools

We live in an age where information is literally at your fingertips, making due diligence easier than ever. Here are some essential tools to make your due diligence efforts easier:

1. **County Government Sites**
   - Assessors, clerks, treasurers, and maps – these are your go-to sources for information. Most counties have websites where you can access property records, tax information, and other critical data.
2. **Google Earth**
   - An amazing application that allows you to virtually visit properties without ever leaving your home. You can get a sense of the land's topography, size, its surroundings, and even potential access issues.

3. **Other Tools**

    - Depending on your needs, there are plenty of other virtual tools and databases that can help you get the information you need. Always keep exploring and updating your toolbox.

Phase 1: Initial Screening

This phase is all about quick evaluation. You're looking for deal-breakers that tell you whether it's worth moving forward with this property.

1. **Ownership Status**

    - Is the person you're dealing with actually the owner of the property? You can verify this through county assessor records. Get a copy of the latest deed on file—it's a simple but crucial step.

    - **Authority to Sell**

- Does the person have the legal right to sell the property? Watch out for multi-ownership issues, deceased spouses, or partners, or if the seller is an authorized trust manager. These factors can complicate or even invalidate a sale.
- Sometimes multiple parties will be 'co-owners.' This definitely complicates the process and can grind it to a halt. But it can also be a competitive advantage if you've got the time and drive to help someone navigate through it all.

2. **Property Access**

   - Does the property have clear, legal access? Landlocked properties can be a nightmare unless you know how to navigate the access issues. Generally, I advise avoiding these unless you have experience or a plan to resolve access problems.

- Checking in with owners of adjacent properties to assess their interest in adding to their land holdings is a great option for properties like this. It can be an easy score.

3. **Financial Issues**

- Are there back taxes owed on the property? If so, how much? This is crucial because it can affect your profit margins or even lead to legal complications if not addressed.
- Also check if the property is in an HOA or LOA as the cost of dues can eat into profit margins, limit the pool

of potential buyers and in the worst case have an accumulation of unpaid dues for which you could become liable.

Phase 2: Final Due Diligence

If the property passes Phase 1, then things are looking good! It's time to roll up your sleeves and dig deeper.

1. **Liens on the Property**
    - Are there any liens that could complicate your ownership? This could include tax liens or other financial obligations tied to the property.
2. **HOA or LOA Dues**
    - Is the property part of a Homeowners Association (HOA) or Landowners Association (LOA)? There could be

accumulated dues owed, which might not be a deal-breaker, but they can definitely eat into your profit margins and might need to be renegotiated. If you haven't checked this as part of Phase 1, definitely make sure now.

3. **Due Diligence Checklist**
    - To make this process quick and easy, we offer a complete due diligence checklist for our coaching students. This checklist is a step-by-step guide to ensure you cover all your bases before closing a deal.

Conclusion

Due diligence isn't just important—it's critical. Here's why:

1. **Critical Importance**

  - Without it, you're essentially gambling with your money. Due diligence gives you the confidence to move forward with a deal, knowing that you've done everything possible to mitigate risks.

2. **Initial Check for Deal-Breakers**
  - Always perform an initial check for any deal-breakers before you invest too much time or money into a property.

3. **Validate and Renegotiate**
  - Use the information you gather during due diligence to validate your offer or renegotiate the deal if necessary. This can save you thousands of dollars and a lot of headaches.

4. **Any Property Can Be a Good Deal…for the Right Price**

- We've never lost money on a deal because we've mastered the art of finding the right price on the right properties. Remember, beauty is in the eye of the beholder. The ugliest, nastiest properties all have someone that will love them and pay you for them.

5. **Title Companies or Abstractors**

- Title companies or abstractors can provide peace of mind, especially when the numbers make sense. The cost of these services should ideally be less than 10% of your profit margins. Whenever possible, get the seller to cover these costs, and if not, split them. Or if the margins are big and juicy as with most of these deals, it's still in your best interest to foot the bill. Remember, pigs get fat. Hogs get slaughtered.

Chapter 11: Time to Do the Deed! (How to Close a Deal)

Congratulations! You've done your research, found the perfect piece of land, and negotiated a great deal. Now, it's time to finalize this acquisition and close the deal. After all, a deal is just a deal until the paperwork is done. This part of the process can seem daunting at first but, once you've got the hang of it, it's a smooth and satisfying process that enables you to bring in top profits, but first things first.

In this chapter, I'll walk you through the different ways of closing on a land purchase. I'll also share my personal recommendations to help you cut down the timeline and maximize profits. By the end of this, you'll have the confidence and knowledge to close deals like a pro.

Different Methods to Close on Land Purchases

There are two primary methods for closing a land deal: using a Title company or handling it everything directly.

1. **Through a Title Company (Hands-off, Sacrifices Profit)**

   When you leverage a Title company, they take care of the heavy lifting for you, from researching the title history to managing the funds in escrow. It's a hands-off approach that provides peace of mind, but it comes with a cost—typically between $500 and $1,500 per transaction. That's money coming out of your pocket, and depending on the size of the deal, that hit to your profits can be significant. On smaller deals, this might not be the best route.

Title companies typically add time to the process. Depending on the company and branch location, this may range anywhere from a week to six or more. While this might not kill a deal or your business, it can unnerve sellers and slow down your cash flow engine.

2. **Manage It Directly (Hands-on, Maximizes Margins)**

   This is the preferred method. By handling the closing yourself, you save on the costs associated with Title companies and keep more of the profits. Yes, it's more hands-on, but the process is relatively simple once you understand it. More importantly, it maximizes your margins, which is what flipping land is all about.

On top of all that, you can drastically cut down the timeline. There will be time allocated to checking chain of title, paperwork such as deeds and any required addendums, and filing; however, most of that can be automated. Many of our closings happen in days and we leverage both the cost and time savings with sellers, so they know it's possible to get cash in their hands quickly.

Why We Prefer Direct Closing

In most cases, we prefer to handle the closing ourselves and cut out the middleman. Here's why:

Value vs. Cost: Title companies add value, no doubt about it. They handle the title search, manage escrow, check for tax liens, and provide title insurance. These are all important functions. But when it comes to flipping land, especially on deals with smaller margins, those costs can eat into your profits quickly. On larger deals, where the profit potential is higher, the cost may be justified. But on smaller flips, it's often worth the extra work to manage things yourself.

Simple and Safe: Direct closing is surprisingly simple in most cases. As long as you've done your due diligence (which we covered in the last chapter), and you know what's required, you can confidently handle the process yourself. With a great checklist and resources at hand, you can close your land deals smoothly and safely, keeping more of your profits in the process.

Step-by-Step: Closing a Deal Yourself

Let's break down the direct closing process step-by-step, so you can see just how manageable it is:

1. **Perform Due Diligence**

   Before you close, ensure all key aspects of the deal are verified and in order. This means checking ownership status, legal access, and any back taxes or liens. Use the checklist introduced in the previous chapter to stay on top of things. Again, your most important deal breakers are around the chain of title (ownership transfer history) and any financial burdens or claims against the property (liens, back taxes, debts, etc.)

2. **Create a Deed**

You'll need a deed for the property owner to sign, transferring ownership to you. There are various templates online but be sure to use the correct one for your state or county. A helpful resource can be the county clerk's office directly. There is almost always information on the county websites that define exactly how deeds should be formatted, example deeds as well as any necessary forms that will be required upon filing. Another resource that can be very helpful is a site: www.deeds.com . They've pulled together an extensive collection of all the required paperwork and items necessary by county. You can purchase single items or packages, saving you time in the process.

3. **Deliver the Deed for Execution**

Once you have the deed, the owner will need to sign in the presence of a notary. This can be done in person or remotely using a mobile notary, which is often more convenient for both parties.

4. **File the Executed Deed with the County**

After the owner signs the deed, it needs to be filed with the appropriate County Department, typically the County Clerk. Each county may have different requirements—some need specific formatting or additional forms. Make sure to check these before filing.

Pro Tip: We love using **SimpliFile**, a third-party web-based platform that allows you to file deeds with counties quickly and easily. Once you've uploaded your paperwork, it often gets recorded within a few hours. It saves time, hassle, and the risk of making a mistake.

5. **Pay the Sellers Once the Deed is Recorded**

   In 99% of direct closings, you'll hold payment until the deed is officially recorded. Once recorded, there are several ways to pay sellers, ranging from mailing/overnighting a check, to electronic payment apps to wiring the funds. Occasionally there are sellers that feel more comfortable with a third-party holding the payment until they've signed over the land, and that's okay. But if you walk them through the process confidently, most sellers will agree to your terms if they feel that's just the normal process.

6. **Voila! Your Deal is Done**

Once the deed is recorded and payment is submitted, you're officially the proud owner of a new parcel of land. The best part? You're ready to flip it for profit and put the process on repeat.

Tips for Closing

Now that you know the process, let's talk about how to decide which closing method to use and how to handle the transaction like a pro.

1. **When to Use a Title Company vs. Direct Closing**

   The decision between using a Title company or managing the deal yourself often comes down to two key factors:

   Profit Margin:

   For deals where the expected profit is less than $4,000, I recommend direct closing to avoid sacrificing your margins. But for deals with larger profits, it's worth considering a Title company for added security and peace of mind.

Seller's Comfort Level:

Sometimes, the seller insists on going through a Title company. When that happens, I'll first try to get them to cover 100% of the cost. If that doesn't work, I'm willing to split the cost 50/50 as long as the profit margin makes sense. If the deal is profitable enough, we'll go through the Title company, even if it means covering the full cost ourselves.

2. **Time Considerations**

Sometimes, using a Title company or other experts can be a time-saver, especially when you're juggling multiple deals. If time is more valuable than money at that moment, it may be worth paying for the convenience.

3. **Confidence is Key**

   When handling the closing process yourself, confidence is critical. Know your processes inside and out. Be clear and direct with the seller about how the transaction will work and lead them through it like the professional you are. When you project confidence, the seller will feel comfortable, and the deal will move forward smoothly.

Closing Thoughts

Successfully navigating the closing process is a huge accomplishment, but it's only the beginning. Now, the real fun begins—flipping that land for a profit and moving on to the next deal! With each successful closing, your confidence will grow, and the process will become second nature.

And remember, whether you choose to handle things yourself or bring in a Title company, the most important thing is that you close the deal efficiently and profitably. Every successful land flip brings you one step closer to mastering this business and creating the financial freedom you've been working toward.

Now, get out there and make the magic happen!

Chapter 12: Finding Buyers (Marketing)

Once you've acquired a piece of land and are ready to flip it, the next step is finding the right buyer. Without a solid marketing strategy, even the best land deal will sit on the market, tying up your capital and limiting your ability to move on to the next flip. Your best marketing land isn't just about casting a wide net and hoping for the best; it's about precision, understanding your buyer, and maximizing the channels and tools available to you.

Let's dive into the art and science of finding buyers and how you can create an efficient, scalable marketing strategy that works.

Pricing Your Property

Before you start to market your newly acquired property, you need to establish your pricing strategy. There are a few factors that go into determining pricing and it can be highly personal to you and your business needs. Here I'll touch on a few approaches and the general framework to be effective.

> **Wholesale Market Pricing:** the general rule of thumb with the wholesale market is to price properties in between acquisition cost and the market pricing. There can obviously be flexibility with this, and it depends on the actual acquisition cost and your evaluation of the market comps.

For example, let's say you pick up a 5-acre property that normally sells for $10,000 on the open market for $3,000. You'd likely price this on the wholesale market for $6,000 - $7,000 so that you'll make a tidy profit (2x or better!) and the buyer still has some "meat on the bone" to also earn a decent return.

Cash vs Financed Pricing: when you decide to sell direct to consumer on the open market, you have a lot more flexibility with your pricing strategy. In many ways the market will dictate pricing levels; however, with land, you can appreciate a wider range of options than with other asset classes. Primarily this is because it is really challenging for consumers to directly compare multiple parcels as many variables such as, topography, on site features and the buyer's dreams come into play.

Generally, it's best to price land for a full cash transaction in line with other properties on the market, plus or minus as it relates to your needs. These needs can be things like your urgency for the revenue and business strategy. From this cash baseline pricing, think about owner financing from a few different angles.

Firstly, as it relates to the total price with owner financing, you want to ensure you're getting compensated appropriately for your delayed capital. Typically, this is in the form of an interest rate premium. You can base this on your usual return on invested capital (which will be really high in the land business) and/or institutional lending terms on loans for land.

Another option for owner financing is to increase the total price of the land and offer zero percent financing. Then for buyers that bring cash to the table for purchases, you can offer a discount. An example of this strategy would look like this: A 5-acre parcel that typically sells for $20,000 would be advertised as $1,000 down payment, $550/month for 60 months. Cash buyers enjoy a deeply discounted price of $20,000. The financed total payments total $34,000 which is approximately an effective 14% interest rate to the buyer if compared to the $20,000 over 5 years. You are, of course, able to adjust this pricing up or down to meet your desires.

There are a couple of other factors to consider when lining up your pricing. The sooner you can get your capital returned, the better. For example, if you paid $7,000 for the above property, how long will it take you to get your investment back? If sold for the terms laid out your return of capital would happen in less than 11 months. This is a great target and then you're enjoying profits for the next 4 years. Additionally, you want a decent return on investment over the life of the investment. This example nets a 77% annualized return. Not bad at all! But it's far short of the near 300% ROI you could earn from a cash sale. Points to consider.

Marketing Channels

There are several channels available to market your land, and the beauty of it is that you can tailor your approach depending on your budget and goals. Here's a breakdown of the primary channels to consider:

1. **First Stop**

   There are a few go-to channels to consider before you get too far along in the process and depending on your business goals and strategy.

- **The Neighbors:** many times, before we have even closed on a property or at least as soon as we are the official owners, we'll reach out to the owners of the adjacent properties. This can be a quick and easy sale in some instances. On the flip side, we've also picked up an additional property from the neighbors because we've reached out. Make sure to hit this step early!
- **Wholesalers:** there is a robust wholesale market among land flippers. You can buy and sell on the wholesale market. It's a fast and effective way to gain and maintain momentum in your business under certain circumstances. Depending on the deal you made on the buy-side,

you can quickly earn a tidy profit. You won't net as much as you would in the open market, but it cuts out a lot of marketing and time spent interacting with leads.

-

2. **Free Channels**

   Free marketing channels are a great starting point, especially if you're working with a limited budget. These include:

   - **Craigslist**: While often overlooked, Craigslist can be a treasure trove for real estate leads. Many land investors swear by it, using its free listings to reach buyers in specific regions or interest groups.
   - **Facebook Marketplace and Groups**: Social media platforms, especially

Facebook, allow you to tap into local and national groups where land buyers might be looking. It's quick, easy, and most importantly, free.

- **Zillow:** While the features are limited, Zillow gets a lot of traffic across their site for those looking for real estate.
- **Organic SEO (Search Engine Optimization)**: If you have a website, creating content around land flipping or available properties can bring in free traffic over time. The better optimized your site is for search engines, the more likely potential buyers will find you.
- **Other Online Channels:** Creative usage of other platforms like Instagram, TikTok, Snapchat can help you stand out and really target in on specific land buyer types.

3. **Paid Channels**

   Paid marketing can quickly accelerate your buyer acquisition process. These channels are more targeted, allowing you to reach specific buyers:

   - **Google Ads**: With Google Ads, you can target people actively searching for land to buy in specific areas. This is great because it ensures that your marketing dollars are reaching highly qualified buyers.
   - **Facebook Ads**: Facebook's robust targeting features allow you to show your property listings to people who match your ideal buyer profile. You can even target based on location,

interests (e.g., hunting, camping, or off-grid living), and behavior patterns.

- **Land-Specific Platforms**: There are niche platforms like LandWatch, LandFlip, and Land.com, where buyers specifically looking for land deals can find you. While these platforms are paid, they attract serious buyers, which can make the cost worthwhile in many instances.

4. **Self-Controlled Channels**

   The most powerful form of marketing is one where you control the entire ecosystem. Building and nurturing your own list of buyers allows you to sell land directly, without relying on external platforms:

- **CRM (Customer Relationship Management)**: A CRM system helps you manage your leads, ensuring you're following up with potential buyers in a timely and organized manner. It also allows you to segment your list based on location, interests, and buying history. There are many of these out there and new ones coming to market regularly. Think Hubspot, Pipedrive, Follow Up Boss.
- **Email Marketing**: Regular email updates to your list keep your prospects engaged. Whether you're offering new properties, providing market insights, or simply keeping in touch, email marketing remains one of the most effective ways to close deals. Many CRM's have robust email features. There are also systems

that specifically cater to email marketing that you can use.

- **Hosted Community**: Creating your own online community (e.g., through a Facebook Group or other online forum) allows you to gather interested buyers in one place. Over time, this community becomes a pool of potential buyers who trust you and are ready to act when you post a deal.

The Science & Art of Marketing

Marketing is both an art and a science. While there are tried-and-true methods that can be measured and optimized, there's also the human element—the emotional side of marketing—that drives buying decisions. Let's break this down further:

1. **Features & Benefits**
   At its core, marketing is about communicating the features and benefits of

what you're selling. In the use case of land, the features might include:

- **Acreage**: Size matters, but it's not the whole story.
- **Location**: Proximity to amenities, recreational areas, or future developments.
- **Zoning**: Can the land be developed, farmed, or used recreationally?

The **benefits**, on the other hand, tap into what the buyer can **gain** from owning that land—whether it's a future home site, a recreational retreat, or a long-term investment. Be clear on both features and benefits in every listing. Think about the value each feature can deliver to its future owner.

2. **Emotions Drive Buyers**

Real estate, like all sales, is fueled by emotion. Sure, the numbers need to make sense, but what really seals the deal is the emotional connection the buyer makes with the property:

- **A Vision of Escape**: Many land buyers are looking for freedom—a place to escape the hustle and bustle of city life. Whether it's a remote mountain retreat or an off-grid cabin site, you're selling a dream. Tap into those dreams and you can sell for maximum margins.
- **Investment Opportunity**: Others buy land for financial reasons. It's a stable, appreciating asset that they can pass down to future generations.

Your marketing should tap into these emotions. Use imagery, language, and stories that make buyers envision themselves on the land, living the lifestyle they desire.

3. **Know Your Avatar/Ideal Client Profile** Every piece of land appeals to a specific type of buyer. Knowing who your ideal client is—and marketing directly to them—makes all the difference. For example:
    - Recreational land appeals to outdoor enthusiasts, hunters, or campers.
    - Residential development land appeals to families or developers.
    - Off-grid land appeals to people looking for self-sufficiency.

   The clearer you are about your ideal buyer, the easier it becomes to tailor your marketing to their needs, desires, and pain points.

4. **Leverage the Features of Each Platform** Every platform you use for marketing has its own unique features, and leveraging them can make your listings stand out:

- On Facebook or Instagram, use carousel images and stories to create visually engaging content.
- On Craigslist or real estate platforms, use high-quality photos and detailed descriptions.
- Consider video walkthroughs or drone footage to show the land from a bird's-eye view. Video is particularly powerful because it creates an emotional connection and gives buyers a real sense of the land's potential.

5. **Leverage Resources (Realtors, VAs, Automation, AI)**

Don't do everything yourself. You can—and should—leverage outside resources to help with your marketing:

- **Realtors**: Even though you might not be selling houses, realtors often have a list of potential buyers who are interested in land.

- **Virtual Assistants (VAs)**: VAs can help you manage your marketing efforts, from posting listings to managing responses, allowing you to focus on other parts of your business.
- **Automation & AI**: Tools like chatbots, automated email responders, and AI-driven ad platforms can take much of the manual work off your plate, allowing you to scale your efforts without overwhelming yourself.

6. **Stand Out from the Crowds**

   The land market, while less competitive than other real estate sectors, still requires you to stand out. The key is to differentiate your listings from others:

   - **Creative Listings**: Instead of the same old, tired descriptions, inject some creativity into your listings. Use descriptive language that paints a picture of the lifestyle the buyer is investing in.

- **Visuals**: High-quality, compelling visuals set you apart. Use professional photos, videos, and drone footage to show the full potential of your land.

The Goals of Your Marketing Efforts

Primary Goal: Sell Your Property & Profit from Your Flip

The primary goal of any marketing effort is to sell your property. Every action you take, from writing a listing to running an ad, should be focused on attracting the right buyer and moving them toward a purchase decision.

Secondary Goal: Build Your Own Buyer List

Beyond selling the immediate property, one of the best uses of your marketing efforts is to build a self-controlled list of buyers who are interested in future deals. This list is your goldmine. Every time you have a new property, you'll be able to market it directly to people who already know, like, and trust you—cutting down the time and cost of finding buyers.

With your own list of interested landowners (and clients), you are in control of the communication, not some algorithm that changes without notice.

Tips for Marketing Success

1. **Consistency Pays Off**
   Consistency is everything in marketing. It's not enough to post one ad or listing and hope for the best. If you want continued success and scale with your land business, then posting regularly, running consistent

campaigns, and following up with leads is essential. The more consistent you are, the more momentum you'll build over time.

2. **Experiment and Iterate**

   The great thing about today's marketing landscape is that there are so many free and low-cost platforms to experiment with. Don't be afraid to try different strategies and see what works:

   - **Try different headlines or descriptions** in your listings.
   - **Experiment with new platforms** like TikTok or YouTube if your ideal buyer is there.
   - **Test different formats** (like video vs. static images) to see what resonates most with your audience.

Marketing isn't a static process. It evolves over time and iterates with every experiment and success. Be curious, stay flexible, and never stop testing new ways to reach your audience. You hold a property that's a perfect match for someone out there.

Chapter 13: Mastering the Art of Sales

Selling land is not just a transaction and associated sciences of consumer behaviors and buyer psychology, it's an art form. The way you approach each conversation, manage your energy, and guide the process determines your success as much as the product you're selling. Sales, especially in the land business, goes beyond just listing property. It's about connecting with people, addressing their needs, and offering them something valuable in a way that feels natural and genuine. In this chapter, we'll explore the sales process more deeply, looking at the success factors, best practices, and the mindset you need to bring to each encounter.

Sales Success Factors

The first thing you need to understand about sales is that your personal beliefs and mindset can have a direct impact on every sales interaction. The story you tell yourself about money, success, and your own abilities affects how you present yourself and your offer. And in sales, confidence is king. It's also essential to steady and consistent sales over time.

Think about the times you've encountered a salesperson who lacked confidence. Did you trust them? Probably not. Confidence doesn't mean being aggressive or pushy; it means having an unshakeable belief in the value of what you're offering and projecting that belief clearly to the buyer. Then they can choose to purchase or not. It's about being sure of yourself, your process, and the product you're selling with the goal of finding the right buyer.

Your State, Standards and Story

Before diving into sales, take a moment to audit your personal story. What do you believe about your ability to sell? What story are you telling yourself about money and success? If those stories are full of doubt, uncertainty, or fear, they'll bleed into your sales interactions.

Your State: here we refer to your state of mind. How do you approach a sales conversation? Are you feeling anxious or unsure? Or are you in a state of calm, confident readiness? Buyers can sense your energy before you even say a word, so manage your state before every interaction.

Your Standards: Set high standards for how you conduct your sales process. This isn't about pushing a sale no matter what, but about maintaining professionalism, integrity, and the commitment to serve your buyer's needs. You want to be able to listen actively, ask clarifying questions, position your land in a way that resonates strongly and emotionally with the buyer.

Your Money Story

Your personal beliefs about money will shape how you interact with buyers. For example, if you believe that money is hard to come by or that people won't pay for something that seems "too expensive," those beliefs will show up in your interactions. You might underprice your properties, hesitate to ask for the sale, or struggle with negotiating.

A couple of actions you can take that help influence your money story:

- **Audit Your Beliefs**: Take a hard look at what you believe about money and sales.

Are those beliefs helping you close deals, or are they holding you back? Is there particular language or phraseology that you repeatedly use, such as "money doesn't grow on trees" or "we can't afford it."

- **Rewrite Your Story**: Once you identify limiting beliefs, it's time to create a new, more empowering story. Believe that what you're offering is valuable. Believe that there are buyers out there who are willing to pay for that value. Write down your new belief system that you want to exude. Read it to yourself repeatedly and internalize it. This shift in mindset will not only help you close more sales but will also make the process more enjoyable and less stressful.

Set Personal Agreements for Sales Interactions

One of the best ways to approach sales is with a sense of detachment from the outcome. This doesn't mean you don't care about closing the deal. It does mean that you're not emotionally tied to whether the buyer says "yes" or "no." You're not trying to force an outcome. Each sales encounter is an opportunity for learning, growth, and building confidence, regardless of the end result on any particular transaction or interaction.

- **Give the Buyer Permission to Say "No"** This might sound counterintuitive, but allowing the buyer to say "no" takes the pressure off the interaction. It creates a more genuine conversation where the buyer feels free to express concerns, and it helps build trust. Plus, when people feel they have the freedom to say "no," they're often more likely to say "yes." Be open with them and reflect the point that you realize any given piece of land has to be the right fit.
- **Detach from the Outcome** Your goal in every sales interaction should be to guide the buyer toward making the

best decision for themselves, whether that's a "yes" or a "no." By detaching yourself emotionally from the result, you'll be more present in the conversation and better able to meet the buyer's needs. And in some cases, the right decision for the buyer may be to walk away and look for something different.

The Sales Process: Bad and Best Practices

Now let's get into the specifics of how to handle the sales conversation itself. There are some common pitfalls to avoid, as well as best practices that will help you close more deals.

1. **Bad Practices to Avoid**
   - **Dominating the Conversation (Word Vomit)**: This happens when you talk too much and don't give the buyer room to express themselves. Sales isn't about showing off everything you know—it's about

understanding the buyer's needs and guiding them toward a solution.

- **Being Pushy or 'Salesy'**: Nobody likes a pushy salesperson. Being overly aggressive or desperate will only drive buyers away.
- **Being a Know-it-All**: While you should be knowledgeable, coming off as a know-it-all can alienate your buyer. They need to feel heard and understood, not lectured to.

2. **Best Practices**
    - **Maintain Control of the Process**: This doesn't mean dominating the conversation but rather guiding it. Set expectations early on, stay on track, and involve the buyer in the process. A well-structured conversation builds trust and moves the buyer toward a decision.

- **Apply Good Tactics**: Draw on the emotional needs of your prospects. People don't often make purchases based on logic. They buy from emotion. So work hard to understand what are their pain points, and how does your offer solve those? What happens if they don't act? Paint a compelling image of the benefits of buying and the costs of inaction.
- **Proactively Address Objections**: Don't wait for objections to come up—address them head-on. Buyer's remorse? Offer a guarantee. Concerned about affordability? Highlight your owner-financing options. Worried about trust and credibility? Provide testimonials, references, or showcase your social media presence. Transparency is key.

Let them know about any fees or extras upfront.

3. **Close the Sale!**
   - **Be Confident**: If you're not confident in your offer, why should the buyer be? Even if you're feeling a bit unsure, project confidence. Clearly explain the closing process and then **ask for the close**. Many sales are lost simply because the seller never directly asks for the sale.
   - **Instill Urgency**: Properties are in demand. Let your buyer know that. Offer incentives for quick action or a limited-time discount to encourage them to act now.
   - **Counter-Pressure**: Sometimes, taking the sale away can actually make the buyer want it more. Be willing to say, "Maybe this isn't the right time or the property for you,"

and watch how often that spurs buyers into action.

4. **Follow-Up**: Be specific with your follow-up plan. Set timeliness and expectations for the next steps. Whether it's a call in two days or a final decision on Friday, be clear about when and how you'll move forward.
5. **Build Rapport**: Building rapport is about more than just being friendly. It's about showing the buyer that you genuinely care about their needs. Focus on listening to them, understanding their desires, and positioning yourself as a trusted guide.
6. **People Buy from Those They Know, Like, and Trust**: This age-old sales adage is true in every industry. The more you focus on building relationships and being authentic, the more likely buyers are to trust you with their purchase.

Final Thoughts on Sales

Here's the truth: the right buyer is out there for every property you're selling. Your job is to find them, build a connection, and guide them through the process. Sales shouldn't be about trickery or manipulation. It should be about presenting clarity, confidence, and connection.

- **Be Consistent**: Consistency in marketing and sales interactions pays off. The more you show up and stay engaged, the more momentum you'll build over time.
- **Be Sensitive**: Not every lead is the right buyer, and that's okay. Be sensitive to where people are in the buying process, and don't push a sale just because you're eager to close.
- **Be Clear**: Make sure you can clearly explain the entire sales process, from down payments to contracts, and finally the transfer of title. Buyers feel more

comfortable when they understand what's happening and what to expect.

Ultimately, sales is about providing value and solving problems. If you focus on those two things, you'll not only sell more land, but you'll also create long-lasting relationships with your buyers—relationships that lead to repeat business and referrals. Remember, selling land isn't just about the transaction. It's about building a business based on trust, integrity, and delivering value.

Chapter 14: The Entrepreneurial Mindset

When it comes to entrepreneurship, mindset isn't just a factor for success – it's the foundation. Your business can only grow as large as your mindset allows. Whether you're starting out, scaling up, or pushing through the inevitable roadblocks that come with running a business, having a strong, resilient mindset is the key to sustaining success over the long term.

When we began our entrepreneurial journey into Flipping Dirt, mindset was our most challenging aspect. We quickly learned the processes and steps comprising the business. It's a well-structured process comprised of systems and repetition. Nothing overly complicated. Our biggest challenge was in the execution and overcoming the skepticism, doubt, and fear of failure.

And this is true of most undertakings in life. Athletes, relationships, employees, and employers are all influenced most heavily by the health of their mindsets and outlooks on anything.

The mechanics of any business or activity are generally straightforward and easy to learn. It's when our minds get in the way, when our internal dialogue and stories interfere that we face doubt, uncertainty, overcomplication and in the most extreme cases, surrender.

However, the opposite is also true. Our minds can be our most powerful tool and competitive advantage. When acknowledged, harnessed, and cultivated, the immense power of our minds can make us unstoppable. And this is where real progress and growth is rooted.

Our land flipping coach was extremely clinical. He delivered the material efficiently and robotically. Do this, this way. Set up this process. Execute these actions. We struggled with the inner dialogue. Fortunately, I had decades of experience and education in coaching and mindset. Unfortunately, it's really hard to coach yourself. The saying that you can't see the picture when you're inside the frame is oh so true.

So, Ligia and I leaned on each other. We established processes to build awareness; to share our thoughts, emotions, and fears; and to support one another with motivation, encouragement, and accountability. And it's a core element of our coaching programs today. Because that's where success is rooted, and we are committed to successful transformations in our community.

In this chapter, we'll explore the core components of developing an entrepreneurial mindset that will not only help you build your land-flipping business but also shape you into a stronger, more adaptable leader in every aspect of your life. We'll look at how to create a mindset that embraces growth, fosters perseverance, and equips you with the tools you need to overcome challenges.

Let's go!

The Importance of Mindset in Entrepreneurship

Every entrepreneur plays multiple roles—visionary, manager, salesperson, marketer, and sometimes even administrator. Balancing these roles is a constant challenge, and how you think about them will determine how well you perform. Successful entrepreneurs aren't born; they're shaped by the way they think, the beliefs they hold, and the habits they build.

First, let's address one of the most fundamental and critical outlooks to establish: the difference between a **fixed mindset** and a **growth mindset**.

One of my favorite books of all time is "Mindset," by Carol Dweck. This book and its research and fact-based messages fundamentally changed my outlook. I have always had a firm belief in our ability to learn, adapt and grow. However, Dweck expanded my thinking across so many different domains such as parenting and really drilled down into the detailed levels of small but critical things such as the words we use and how they influence our own thoughts and the thoughts of others. I'll share a few key concepts in this dichotomy of mindset here and encourage you to check out her book when and wherever you can.

- **Fixed Mindset**: This is the belief that your abilities, talents, and intelligence are static. People with a fixed mindset often fear failure because they see it as a reflection of their innate abilities. They have thoughts and beliefs like we are born with a certain capacity for intelligence; have innate skills with maximum ceiling of potential (like golfing or running); or have a defined level creativity for art, music, etc.

- **Growth Mindset**: On the other hand, a growth mindset believes that anything can be learned and improved. It views challenges and failures as opportunities for learning. Those with a growth mindset believe that their abilities can be developed through hard work, dedication, and learning. And research proves that entrepreneurs who adopt a growth mindset are more adaptable, resilient, open to change and ultimately successful.

Developing a Growth Mindset

Once an awareness and understanding of the difference is clear, the next step in developing your growth mindset is understanding that failure is not the end result, it's just feedback. As an entrepreneur, you're going to face obstacles and setbacks. Some deals will fall through, some strategies won't work, and some days will feel overwhelming. But that's part of the process. It's an input that can be used to adjust course…or not. Every successful entrepreneur has failed at some point, and it's their mindset that determined whether they stayed down or got back up.

Here are some strategies for developing and maintaining a growth mindset:

1. **Embrace Failure as Feedback**: Failure is a necessary ingredient for success. Each misstep teaches you something that moves you closer to your goal. Again, the book "Mindset" by Carol Dweck explains how embracing failure is crucial for growth. The key is to see every setback as a steppingstone to progress, not a reason to

quit.

2. **Build Resilience and Grit**: Resilience is the ability to bounce back after adversity. Getting back on that horse when you fall off. Yeehaw! Grit is the perseverance to keep going, even when the road is tough. Keep running when you hit the marathon wall at mile 20.

"The Gap and the Gain" by Dan Sullivan and Dr. Benjamin Hardy is another incredible book that teaches us to focus on how far we've come (the gain) rather than how far we still need to go (the gap). As driven people with big goals, it's easy to get caught up in always looking to the next milestone or target. But this simple shift in focus where we pause now and again to celebrate progress can fuel you to keep moving forward.

3. **Adopt a Learning Mindset**: Every day is an opportunity to learn. The most successful entrepreneurs are those who constantly seek to improve themselves and their business. Books like "10x Is Easier Than 2x" by Hardy & Sullivan challenge you to think bigger and expand your vision by adopting strategies that multiply your results, rather than simply working harder. And staying abreast of new systems, tools and technologies helps keep businesses competitive and outperforming the competition. Be an endless learner…but apply what you learn!

Big Visions and Goal-Setting

Your mindset is also the lens that determines the clarity of your vision and the goals you set. If you approach goal setting with a limited mindset and a sense of scarcity, you'll set small, incremental goals and severely limit what you can achieve. But if you embrace a mindset of abundance and possibility, your goals will reflect that, and your potential results will be that much greater.

Set Big, Audacious Goals

Tony Robbins is one of the greatest coaches in the world and helps millions of people achieve their best. One of the key concepts he's known for is his RPM (Results, Purpose, Massive Action Plan) system, which teaches entrepreneurs to set big, visionary goals and work backward to create a clear plan of action. A key element of the system, however, is purpose. When you link the result you want, your goal, to an unstoppable reason or element of purpose, then you will create an action plan to overcome any obstacle in your way. What you NEED to achieve is paired with why you MUST achieve it.

Coming from a related, but slightly different angle, the 10x concept is widely used in business and coaching. In Dan Sullivan's book "10x Is Easier Than 2x," he and Dan Hardy challenge you to think ten times bigger than what you think is possible. The concept here is that if you set a goal to grow by two times, or incrementally, your solutions tend to be merely doing more of what you already are. You can simply increase whatever is working for you currently – put in more time, add another person, cram in more clients.

But by setting big, audacious, 10x goals, you stretch your capabilities. You have to look for totally different solutions. Paradigm shifts that don't involve "more of the same" but rather tap into ideas and concepts that need to be unique. In this way you position yourself for exponential growth.

Use Time Management Wisely

Another critical aspect of mindset is how you think about and manage your time. When we began our land business journey, we adopted the **12-Week Year** concept, as popularized by Brian Moran in his book of the same name. This methodology teaches entrepreneurs to treat every 12 weeks as a full year, breaking down long-term goals into achievable weekly actions. When you plan yearly goals, your mind can see them as far away and less urgent until you get to the last few months and realize that you're way off course and unlikely to achieve what you set out to accomplish. Keeping your targets in quarterly, or 12-week increments allows you to create more urgency and remain focused on what matters most. You're also able to course correct more quickly when and if you do drift so that you're better able to hit those annual goals and targets.

Metrics and Dashboards

Once you've set your big goals, it's critical to track your progress. Using metrics and dashboards helps you measure what's working and what needs adjustment. Having a clear, visual representation of your progress keeps you motivated and on track. It's easy to overdo this area and try to measure everything. My recommendation is to identify those elements that are directly within your control (how many offers you send out, how many ads placed, etc.) and to focus on a few critical indicators.

Overcoming Fear and Self-Doubt

Let’s face it: fear and self-doubt are some of the biggest obstacles for entrepreneurs. Whether it’s fear of failure, fear of rejection, or simply the fear of the unknown, these emotions can hold you back if you let them. But, just like any other mindset challenge, fear and self-doubt can be overcome with the right strategies.

When we started out, this was one of our biggest and most challenging obstacles to work through. Fortunately, we had strong partners in each other and a strong desire (our ‘why’) to make this path in life work for us. We DID NOT want to have to go back to working for someone else and relying on them for a paycheck. Here are a few of the methods we used to overcome our fears:

Identify Limiting Beliefs

Often, our fears are rooted in limiting beliefs—those thoughts that tell us we're not good enough, smart enough, or capable enough. These beliefs shape how we show up in our businesses. By identifying these beliefs, you can start the work of reframing them into something more empowering. This requires setting aside time for reflection and introspection. Grab a fresh journal and settle in with yourself. A great coach can also work wonders in this area.

Reframe Limiting Beliefs

Our minds are powerful and work hard to align with our belief system. However, like a computer or phone, they can be reprogrammed. So, once you have your limiting beliefs identified, rewrite them! Consciously and intentionally create the story that you want to have. It will take some time, but if you work daily to internalize your new and improved storyline, you'll soon see significant change. A great way to do this is to read aloud to yourself your new story. You need to have belief however to really make this work.

The concept of a **Money Story** is a perfect example of how limiting beliefs can shape your behavior. We all have a 'story' of how we think about money. Our upbringing instills certain concepts of it. We hear our parents and others talk about it (or avoid it!). "Money doesn't grow on trees!" "We can't afford that."

We live an experience as children and adults. If you believe that money is scarce or hard to come by, that belief will affect how you price your services, negotiate deals, and manage your finances. But by auditing that story and reframing it, you can shift your relationship with money to one of abundance and flow. You can find many great exercises and examples online of how to review and rewrite your money story.

Build Confidence Through Small Wins

Confidence isn't something that magically appears for most of us. It's built through a series of small successes. In Dan Sullivan's books **4Cs Formula**, he outlines how confidence comes from making a **Commitment,** taking **Courageous Action**, which then leads to expanded **Capability** and then to increased **Confidence**. Every time you push through fear and take action, you're building your confidence muscles. It's a very simple framework that elegantly shows how this feedback loop can be used to grow your confidence in any situation.

Resilience and Perseverance in Entrepreneurship

Building a successful business requires both resilience and perseverance. As the adage goes, it doesn't matter how many times you fall; it's about how many times you get back up. Developing these traits as an entrepreneur is essential if you want to succeed in the long term. Some helpful actions in building resilience are:

Maintain a Positive Mindset in the Face of Challenges

Life and business are full of challenges. The question isn't whether you'll face obstacles, it's how you'll handle them when they arise. Maintaining a solution-oriented mindset, rather than dwelling on the problem, is key to persevering through tough times. Find ways to anchor your outlook on the goal, the progress you have and are making, and use obstacles along the way as learning moments to adjust your actions and achieve your goals.

Develop a Support System

No entrepreneur should go it alone. Surround yourself with mentors, peers, and a support system that can motivate and hold you accountable when the going gets tough. One of the biggest myths in entrepreneurship is that you have to do everything yourself. The truth is, building a network of support is essential for resilience.

Embrace Setbacks and Failures

The most successful entrepreneurs aren't the ones who never fail, they're the ones who keep going after failure. By adopting a growth mindset, you can view every setback as an opportunity to learn and improve. This is an outlook I've struggled with and worked hard to reframe. In fact, I don't even like to use the word "failure". Failure to me is not trying something at all. Not listening to your inner voice, your hopes, and your dreams. Everything else when done in pursuit of something is a data point along the way.

Mindset for Long-Term Success

Finally, it's important to adopt a mindset for long-term success. Building a business is a marathon, not a sprint. You'll need a mindset that aligns with both your short-term goals and your long-term vision.

Stay Aligned with Your Core Values

One of the most important aspects of long-term success is ensuring that your business aligns with your personal values. Your business should be a reflection of what you believe and the impact you want to make in the world. When your actions align with your values, you'll feel more fulfilled and motivated to keep pushing forward.

Early on in my journey, I enlisted a coach. He took me through an exercise to brainstorm a list of values that were important to me and then rank them all in order. I now incorporate them in a Life Blueprint. This document contains my core values, my life purpose statement, long-term goals, more immediate goals, and a few other important items such as affirmations, growth focus areas and key actions I'm working on. I review this formally each year, adjust it quarterly and refer to it (or at least try to) daily. It's been instrumental in my long-term growth and development.

Adopt a CEO Mindset

As your business grows, your role will need to evolve. Adopting a CEO mindset means focusing on strategic decision-making, delegation, and building a team that can carry out your vision. You can't do everything yourself, nor should you. Focus on the tasks that drive the most value and let others handle the rest. It may take time to build up to this level, but it should be present from the start. Life is about your experiences and time freedom is what this business is all about. So don't trade one job for another. Build something that gives you more freedom.

Focus on Long-Term Success

Building a sustainable business requires consistent effort and a focus on long-term goals. This is where the concepts of a **self-managing company**, and hiring the right team members, come into play. By focusing on building a great reputation, cultivating raving fans, and creating systems that allow your business to run smoothly without your constant oversight, you're setting yourself up for success far into the future.

Mindset isn't just an element of entrepreneurship, it's the cornerstone of success. By developing a mindset that celebrates growth, embraces failure, and fosters resilience, you'll position yourself to not only build a profitable business but also enjoy the process of entrepreneurship. It's not always easy, but with the right mindset, anything is possible.

Chapter 15: Becoming "Filthy Rich"

When we talk about becoming "filthy rich," it's not really about the money. In fact, money is only a fraction of the equation. An enabler. True wealth, how we define it and what we're ultimately seeking, is about creating a life filled with richness in all domains of life. Richness of experiences; richness of relationships, time, and meaning. This chapter is about redefining what it means to be rich and how you can use your land-flipping business to achieve that richness in all areas of your life.

Redefining "Rich": It's More Than Money

Most people equate being rich solely with financial wealth. But if you take a moment to consider the people who seem to have it all, is it because they're financially wealthy, or is there something more? For me, Ligia, and the truly successful people I've met, being rich is about living a life that feels abundant in every way. That's where the true fulfillment lies. Money is a key enabler, but it's only a very small portion of the lifestyle. Let's break down this broader definition of what it means to be "filthy rich."

Richness of Experiences

We only get one life here on earth! Life is meant to be lived, not just spent working and surviving. True wealth allows you to collect experiences: traveling to new places, engaging in hobbies you're passionate about, learning new things, and making memories with the people you love. Richness of experiences is the ability to pursue the things that light you up, whether that's hiking through the Rockies, exploring new cities, spending quiet weekends by the lake or simply having an enjoyable conversation with friends.

Richness of Relationships

What's money without people to share it with? One of the greatest indicators of a rich life is the quality of your relationships. Whether it's deep connections with family, strong friendships, or an inspiring network of like-minded entrepreneurs, wealth is also measured by the support and love you receive from the people in your life. I believe in the Law of Reciprocity, which to me means that the amount of love and support you receive is dependent on what you give. So, focus on adding richness to your relationships, rather than taking, and you'll always be fulfilled.

Richness of Time

Time is the one resource we can never get back. In the traditional 9-to-5 grind, we trade our time for money, but what if you could break free from that cycle? Real wealth is having the ability to choose how you "spend" your time. Being able to decide whether you invest time in working on your business, spending time with loved ones, or pursuing personal growth. When you control your time, you control your life and are truly rich.

Richness of Meaning

Finally, a life of filthy riches is one filled with purpose and meaning. This is more than just earning a paycheck, hitting financial goals, and buying material things. It's about making a difference, whether in your community, in the lives of your family, or on an even larger scale. It's about waking up with a sense of purpose, knowing that what you're doing matters and adding value. Leave the world a better place for having been in it.

Purpose and Meaning: The True Drivers of Wealth

Money, as important as it is, is not the sole driver of a fulfilling life. Yes, we need money to meet our basic needs, like food, shelter, security; but beyond that, we have the freedom to pursue a richer life. And it's this freedom that allows us to seek out and define our purpose and meaning.

This Is More Profound Than Money

We've all heard stories of people who have

achieved great financial success only to find themselves unhappy. This is the difference in success and fulfillment. Money alone cannot fill the deeper voids in our lives. It's a means to ends. Being filthy rich means understanding what gives you purpose and aligning your life with those values. Whether it's creating a legacy for your family, giving back to your community, or simply having the time to enjoy the things that matter most to you, purpose and meaning are the true indicators of a wealthy life.

Money Is Essential, But It's a Means, Not an End

Let's not discount the importance of money. It's the fuel that drives your journey. But once your basic needs are met, money becomes only a tool for creating the life you want. It allows you to buy back your time, pursue your passions, and make an impact in the areas you care about. It's not the destination—it's the vehicle that takes you where you want to go.

Beyond Money: Richness in Other Areas When we free ourselves from the constant worry of making ends meet, we can begin to focus on the other areas of our lives that bring richness. That might be deepening relationships, exploring new hobbies, or simply enjoying the freedom that comes from financial security. The goal is to create an abundance in all aspects of life, not just in your bank account.

A World of Filthy Riches Awaits You

Here's the exciting part: we live in a world full of opportunity! With the right mindset and strategies, you can create a life of abundance, freedom, and yes, wealth. But it all starts with believing that this kind of life is possible for you. You are the author of your own book, and every decision you make is a new chapter in your journey.

This life is incredible! When you step back and realize the opportunities that exist today, it's almost mind-blowing. We're living in a time where entrepreneurship is more accessible than ever before. The digital age has broken down barriers, allowing people like you and me to create businesses that fit our lifestyles—businesses that generate wealth, provide value, and give us the freedom to live life on our terms.

And because of all of that, you can easily be the author of your own life. You are not a passive participant in your own life. You have the power to design a life that reflects your values, desires, and goals. Land flipping is one of those vehicles that can accelerate your journey toward financial freedom and allow you to create the life you've always dreamed of. But it requires action. You need to take that first step toward building something bigger than yourself.

The Formula to be Filthy Rich: Create Passive Income That Exceeds Your Expenses

The formula is simple: create enough income, passively, if possible, to cover your expenses, and you'll unlock the door to financial and lifestyle freedom. This is the ultimate goal. Once your passive income covers your living costs, you are free to spend your time however you choose. That's the beauty of land flipping. By consistently buying and selling vacant land, you can build a stream of income that works for you, even when you're not actively working.

And once you've created that baseline of financial security, you can accelerate your journey. Whether that means expanding your business, investing in new ventures, or simply enjoying more of life, the opportunities are endless. But it all starts with creating that foundation of passive income. That's the accelerant to wealth accumulation.

Time = The Ultimate Freedom

As we've discussed, there's one thing that money can buy that's more valuable than anything else: time. Time is the ultimate freedom, and it's the one resource we can't create more of. So, how do you maximize it?

1. **Freedom of Money**

   Financial freedom isn't just about having more money—it's about having enough money to make choices. It's about not being tied to a 9-to-5 job, about not stressing over bills, and about being able to invest in the things that matter most to you.

2. **Freedom of Choice**

   When you're financially secure, you have the freedom to make choices that align with your values. You can choose how you spend your time, who you spend it with, and what projects you pursue. This is the freedom that comes from financial independence.

3. **Freedom of Relationships**

   One of the greatest gifts that comes with wealth is the ability to invest in the relationships that matter most. When you're not consumed by the grind, you have the time and energy to nurture your relationships with family, friends, and colleagues.

4. **Freedom of Location**

   In today's world, we're no longer tied to one location for work. Whether you want to live by the beach, in the mountains, or travel full-time, financial freedom gives you the ability to live where and how you want.

This is what we mean by becoming "filthy rich." It's not only about accumulating financial wealth.

It's focused on creating a life that's rich across the important areas of our lives. That richness is enabled by taking control of your finances, but it doesn't have to start or end there. You are ultimately in control of the level of richness you experience in this life. Maximize it!

And by building a business that creates passive income, you can unlock the doors to a life full of experiences, relationships, time, and meaning.

This is exactly what our **Flipping Dirt Coaching Program** (https://flippingdirt.us/landbaron/) is designed to help you achieve. We're not just teaching you how to flip land. We're helping you build a life of abundance, freedom, and purpose.

The opportunities are there, waiting for you.

All you have to do now…is take the first step!

Additional Resources

Dig in deeper: https://flippingdirt.us/

Life: Elevated on YouTube:
https://www.youtube.com/@mikeandligia

Cash Flow Fight Club podcast:
https://cashflowfightclubpod.podbean.com/

Connect with me on LinkedIn:
https://www.linkedin.com/in/michaelbdeaton/

Acknowledgements

Writing this book and building the life I've dreamed of would not have been possible without the incredible support, guidance, and inspiration I've received along the way. I owe a deep debt of gratitude to many who have contributed to my journey, both in land flipping and in life.

First and foremost, to my parents: You instilled in me a strong work ethic, teaching me the importance of character and the way we treat others. You showed me the value of leading with integrity and always respecting the diversity of all life. Those early lessons shaped the person I am today and have provided a foundation for everything I've built. Your unwavering belief in me has carried me through countless challenges, and for that, I am eternally grateful.

To the coaches and mentors who have influenced my life and business: Thank you for sharing your wisdom, for pushing me to grow beyond what I thought possible, and for providing guidance when I needed it most. Whether in formal coaching relationships or through lessons from the industry's thought leaders, your impact has been monumental. Your influence has helped shape my approach to both land investing and living a life of purpose.

To my wife, Ligia: There are no words that can truly express the depth of my gratitude for your unwavering and unconditional support. You encourage me to pursue greatness, even when the path is uncertain, and your belief in me never wavers. You are my biggest inspiration, my fiercest supporter, and the light that keeps me moving forward. Every success I've achieved in this chapter of our lives, I owe in large part to your love and encouragement.

To my family, friends, and those who believed in me, even when the dream seemed distant or improbable: Your words, your faith, and your cheerleading have meant more than you could ever know. To the community of land flippers and entrepreneurs who have shared stories, strategies, and support: Thank you for reminding me that we're all in this together, striving to build lives of abundance and meaning.

To my readers: Thank you for taking the time to invest in this journey with me. Your willingness to explore the world of land flipping and to pursue the dream of financial freedom and a life of purpose inspires me every day. Writing this book was driven by the hope that it would ignite a spark within you, encouraging you to take bold steps toward the life you envision. I am deeply grateful for your trust in me and for giving me the opportunity to share my experiences and insights. Your ambition, curiosity, and dedication to creating a life of abundance are what make this work meaningful. I hope this book empowers and motivates you as you embark on your own path to success.

And finally, thank you all for allowing me to be part of your journey. It is one of my greatest desires to make an impact, however large or small, during my time on this earth.

About the Author

Mike Deaton is a seasoned entrepreneur, investor, real estate coach, and the founder of the Flipping Dirt coaching program, where he works with aspiring freedom fighters to help them achieve financial freedom through the art of flipping vacant land.

Having spent decades running Operations, global supply chains, and earning his MBA; Mike also is a certified coach, having studied under Tony Robbins and Chloe Madanes. Mike combines strategic business acumen with a deep understanding of personal development to help his clients transform not only their financial futures but also their personal outlook.

When he's not flipping dirt or coaching others to success, Mike can be found on the trails at home in Colorado drawing as much as he can out of life together with his wife, Ligia. His commitment to personal growth, adventure, and making a positive impact drives every chapter of his work, both on and off the page.

www.ingramcontent.com/pod-product-compliance
Lightning Source LLC
Chambersburg PA
CBHW052314220526
45472CB00001B/111

* 9 7 9 8 3 0 0 5 4 3 9 3 8 *